# Walking On Air

### How to face challenges with resilience and adversity with strength

### by Francis O' Toole

*For my mum, Phyllis Quinlan O' Toole, a champion of Christianity.*

# Contents

# Acknowledgements

To my three children, Zoe, Micah and Leon (stepson); thank you for the gift of being, for the fun, laughter and memories.

To my family and friends, thank you for caring and sharing.

For the people of Templemore, County Tipperary and County Meath.

All profits from the proceeds of this book will go to the Peter McVerry Trust, a charity set up by Fr. Peter McVerry to reduce homelessness and the harm caused by drug misuse and social disadvantage.

# 1. The Hero's Journey

We all love stories.

Joseph Campbell studied stories across cultures and across history. He identified a common thread in many of the stories we tell ourselves, in the books we read and the films we watch. He called it the hero's journey. The key components of the hero's journey include:

1. Having a yearning for change, for adventure, for a more meaningful life;
2. Overcoming the challenges faced by departing from the familiar, the land of the known;
3. Encountering and facing challenges, adventures and insights along the journey;
4. Struggling with and finally overcoming one or many major ordeals;
5. Obtaining enormous benefit at the end of the journey.

The individual who perseveres and overcomes the various challenges of the hero's journey, who transcends his/her limitations and reaches a new level of existence where all manner of things are possible, is transformed into something better. The hero is a role model for us all.

Life itself is a story: it has a clear beginning — birth — and a clear ending — death. In between those two great thresholds, we journey with the great teacher: life itself. This teacher, life, brings each of us on a great adventure: for me this is awakening. Awakening is when we have a deep experience. Something happens to us. We listen and reflect and know we cannot go back to the old way. You know something deep within has changed and it allows you to have a different perception and outlook on life.

Well, life experience presents us with challenges, encourages us to take risks from time to time and introduces us to many people. Over the course of our journey, our emotions experience great highs and lows. We experience sadness and joy, poverty and richness, loneliness and friendship.

This book is my story: my journey with the teacher of life. I walk and talk with every person who is willing to share this journey, I listen and empathise with others, and I share some of my highlights and some of my pain and brokenness. I allow the events of my life to teach me lessons so that I can gain insight and move forward, always learning.

I invite you to reflect on your stories and experiences. I want you to embrace all of them and take ownership of them believing we are all heroes. Someday you too will share your story with family, friends and loved ones. Finally, my wish is that each person who reads this book will be inspired to reach their full potential, be happy and flourish. In stillness and silence, much can be discovered about the great teacher: life itself.

# 2. Walking On Air Against My Better Judgment

### *"Walk On Air Against Your Better Judgment"*
from '*The Gravel Walks*' by Seamus Heaney
(also inscribed on his gravestone at Bellaghy, County Derry).

I ponder those words and try to work out what Seamus is saying to us. I find the words inspirational. To me, the idea of 'walking on air' touches off the Divine, while still staying firmly rooted to the ground. It's about 'going for it', creating a dream or vision and believing: "Yes, I can do this." As an Irishman, I am generally cautious. Maybe this is true of most people. I often tend to be self-judgmental, building up stories and reasons in my head as to why I cannot do certain things. In other words, making excuses. Seamus is suggesting that we throw caution to the wind. He is encouraging us to be open to risk-taking, not to be inhibited, not to be held back.

As I stood at his graveside in Bellaghy, time passed. I became more relaxed and had a sense that I was on sacred ground. I began to speak to Seamus. I told him my story. I shared my life's journey. I told him about the ups and downs, the pains, struggles, disappointments, heartbreak, sickness, loneliness, achievements and the happy times with the people I had met on my journey. I was speaking to a man who had passed on. A man of fame whom I never met. I had never read his poetry or writings and yet I was transformed in that moment.

One line from Seamus Heaney's poetry was enough to change my world forever. I could hear Seamus saying, *"Francis, do not be afraid, pick up a pen and paper and write your story."* I left that graveyard 'walking on air'. I could feel my blood boiling, the passion of my heart coming alive and my mind creating a new story with a new beginning.

The next day:

- against my better judgement, I purchased a journal;
- against my better judgement, I started to put pen to paper;
- against my better judgement, I began to record some events from my life;
- against my better judgement, I said, *"One day I will produce a book"*;
- against my better judgement, I wrote for forty days: poems and prose.

So, here I am, 'walking on air, against my better judgement'.

# 3. 'I Am'

*"I am not what I ought to be, I am not what I want to be,
I am not what I hope to be in another world; but
still I am not what I once used to be, and by the grace
of God I am what I am."* — John Newton.

In some of the stories here, you will notice the words 'I
Am'. These are powerful words when they are statements
of the soul. This is the belief that the body is a gift from
the world and that the soul is a gift from the Divine.

Our soul is within our being. We cannot see it yet it is so
powerful. Just like the winds of nature, you can't see it,
but never underestimate its strength and power. The Greek
philosophers talked about the existence of the soul before
Christ came on earth. The people of the Old Testament
talked about the soul and how God was slowly revealing
himself to his people over time. People have been speaking
of the soul within the body for thousands of years. In the
New Testament, St. Paul speaks about the body being the
temple of the spirit. Jesus Christ speaks about destroying
the temple and restoring it in three days. Was he speaking
of the destruction of his body and the resurrection of his
soul in three days after his death on the cross? One can
only conclude from this that both the body and soul are
touched by the Divine, since God chose to live in human
form on earth. It would seem to me that the body, mind
and soul need to be cared for to function properly. The
body needs to be enriched with food, water, exercise, rest
and sleep.

Most people will at some stage test their strength in the world of sports and their minds in the halls of fame. But what about the soul? The soul is that which brings our bodies alive. Our souls are the personification of the beauty of God. The soul allows us to be in touch with the Divine. When I spent six years studying in the seminary, the soul was given high value; we nourished the soul daily with meditation, prayer and silence. How many people do you hear shouting from the rooftops that they would like to enrich their soul and allow its light shine for the world to see? We are only comfortable if something is tangible and easily assessed or monitored.

I live in the village of Slane in County Meath near Newgrange, which is a prehistoric monument on the north side of the River Boyne. If you go on a guided tour you will be informed that Newgrange was built during the Neolithic period around 3200 BC, making it older than Stonehenge and the Egyptian pyramids. No one knows for certain what this site was used for, but many would suggest that it had religious significance — it is aligned with the rising sun and the sun's light illuminates the chamber on the winter solstice which normally falls on 21 December. I constantly ask myself is it celebrating light over darkness? Is it a celebration of thanksgiving for the harvest? Every time I visit this site, I sense a powerful atmosphere, a peaceful presence full of wisdom and knowledge. Newgrange is telling us clearly that people in Ireland over 5,000 years ago had a spirituality or a sense that there was something greater than themselves beyond this physical world of earth. It is evidence of humans getting in touch with the spirit world.

After 53 years of living on this earth, I no longer want to believe in the soul that lays dormant in the body until we die. I want to believe in a soul that is always free. I now have a deeper desire to get in touch with the soul, a soul that is fully alive and not trapped in a body.

I now want to challenge my belief systems that it's the body, soul and mind working in harmony that brings us life and endless possibilities. The soul is all of me: my personality, fears, emotions, feelings, imagination, etc. The soul is capable of going far beyond the body or mind. The soul takes on the shape of the body and mind to give it a visible expression to the world we live in.

If we can accept the challenge of allowing time for our soul, our life story will be a mighty adventure from birth to death. Maybe we need to change our conventional ways of getting in touch with the soul. I need to develop a new being; 'I am' allowing the soul to be free to dance with the rhythm of life. I believe we can develop a belief system allowing for the power of 'I am'; this in turn will allow us to experience a touch of the Divine. The soul is easily found in silence, meditation, mindfulness and solitude.

If you develop true silence and solitude you will never experience loneliness or isolation because your spirit is in connection with the universe. This will allow you to discover the real you and seek challenges that go far beyond your expectations or abilities. Hence the longest journey in the world is the journey from the head to the heart. Find your heart's desire: here you will find your soul touching off something greater. Learn to have the ability to state with confidence that the Divine is within.

I would suggest that you repeat the following powerful statements to yourself:

- I am fulfilled and grateful;
- I am a fighter;
- I am a person of faith;
- I am practising self-care;
- I am safe and all around me will be safe;
- I am a mind, body and soul in healing;
- I am one who draws good things into my life;
- I am an amazing person with great strengths and abilities.

Continue making positive statements beginning with 'I am'.

These powerful statements beginning with 'I am' will help change your world for the better.

'I am' confident, comfortable, healing, hopeful, healthy, abundant, wealthy and happy.

'I am' the way, the truth and the light.

# 4. Direction

*"It's the possibility of having a dream come true
that makes life interesting. "* — Paulo Coelho.

We are all looking for direction in life. We get ideas,
wisdom and insights from the experience of others, from
the world around us and from nature. My first job, at the
age of 12, was as an assistant barman in the Templemore
Arms Hotel. Of course this would not be allowed today
because of new legislation. I have to say I learned a lot
watching how people interacted and how people can make
fools of themselves under the influence of alcohol. I was
always impressed with the hotel staff who were committed
to service and cared for the customers with tremendous
respect and loyalty. I watched how the management led,
prepared and organised events; everything was planned
down to the final detail. I was always energised by their
commitment, dedication, time management skills,
administrative skills, cooking skills and so on. The list is
endless. As a teenager I was so inspired by the people I
worked with that I considered hotel management as a
career. I even wanted to leave school after my Junior Cert
as I had secured a place to train with Cert, the body
responsible at that time for hotel management and catering
qualifications.

Of course, thanks to the wisdom of my parents, this did
not happen. I was very disappointed but as I matured I
accepted their reasoning. I continued to work in the hotel
during my Leaving Cert years and then I discovered a

new career. I joined the FCA, now known as the Local Defence Force. I was proud and delighted to wear an army uniform and — would you believe it — I won best recruit award in training! This led to acceptance on a course as a corporal, a non-commissioned officer, at the age of seventeen. Back then lots of young people joined the FCA. As a corporal, I now had two years experience of FCA army training and could use a rifle and machine gun with firing ability of up to 600 rounds a minute.

I now considered joining the army as a way of life. This was no surprise as I had three brothers serving in the army and UN peacekeeping force at that time and five generations of our family, including my Dad, had served in the army.

During the Irish Easter rebellion in 1916 my grandmother May Grogan was arrested as a young teenager and held prisoner for a short period of time for acting as a messenger for the rebels on O'Connell Street, Dublin. Ironically, her father Peter Grogan of the Royal Dublin Fusiliers left his family behind to fight in the trenches of Flanders. Ireland at that time was still under England's rule but England promised to allow Irish Home Rule if enough men volunteered for the war. Over the course of World War I, around 250,000 Irishmen joined the ranks of the British army; unfortunately more than 30,000 died in battle. Peter Grogan was killed in action in 1917, aged 38, at the Battle of Arras in France.

On 11 November, 1922 my grandmother's first cousin, Peter Cassidy of the Irish Republic Army, was executed by firing squad by the Free State Army at Kilmainham Gaol, Dublin. There is a simple plaque in Kilmainham Gaol to remember Peter Cassidy and the three other men who were the first victims of execution in the civil war.

My grandfather, Joseph O' Toole from Swords, Dublin, fought at the Battle of Gallipoli. Tens of thousands of Allied soldiers lost their lives going over the top at Gallipoli. The Irish forces found themselves fighting in intolerable conditions and outnumbered by the Turkish soldiers.

My Mum's father, Patrick Quinlan from Templemore, was awarded the Military Medal for bravery at the Battle of Passchendaele. He was also awarded two citations for bravery in the field during the battles of Arras and the Somme.

Yes, of course I considered the army as a way of life. I believe in honour and strength in unity. But in a strange silent way and due to the powerful influence of my mum, I became very interested in the life of a priest. Mum is a woman of great faith but always had faith in action by doing charitable deeds. I wanted to be an instrument of peace. Most times, direction will come from our experience and family. I served in active ministry for ten years as a priest. While our journey may seem straightforward, a lot of time may be lost feeling lonely, isolated or even on the margins of society, especially when we take a different route than others. When the journey is difficult, believe in the presence of God in your life, guiding and directing your every move. I know I questioned my own faith and belief in God on many occasions but always when I look back on experiences, I can see how God's hand was there guiding and pointing me in a certain direction. This was so true when I talk about my experience with a sick child.

## War and Peace

Times of peace,
Young men
Walk in the shadows
Of their Dads'
Touchstones.

Times of war,
Old men
Talk in the shadows
Of their sons'
Headstones.

# 5. Creativity and Gardening

*"Creativity requires the courage to let go of certainties. "*
— Erich Fromm

I have loved gardening since I was young. I would watch with awe and wonder as my Dad planted seeds in the ground and waited patiently to see what was going to happen. As time passed and I grew older, the seeds would burst into new life and produce amazing, beautiful plants. I was fascinated by the beauty of the flowers. It was interesting to see how different flowers attract different insects, all with their own agenda and mission to complete.

Many years later I entered a seminary to study for the priesthood. During those six years of intensive study with classes six days a week, I was given the opportunity to develop skills in garden work. I was given full responsibility to design and organise a little piece of land as I saw fit. I was allowed to take the initiative and sow seeds which would produce their plants and flowers in due time. During this period the world of gardening became a sanctuary for me to escape to, especially when the pressure of exams in Philosophy and Theology was on the horizon. The gardening kept me grounded.

Later in life I was fortunate to live by the sea with my young family and when we first moved in, the existing garden was full of trees. I never added anything to the garden. I just watched the trees grow every year and every year I trimmed them. Eventually I realised that I wanted my own garden full of shrubs and flowers planted according to my design. Still knowing little about horticulture, I began to research plants and shrubs and began to take a more active interest in programmes and articles about gardening. I then went and planted the garden I wanted. There is a little pond for insects, frogs and whatever nature provides. Now it is a garden full of secret passageways and little footpaths, like a maze. It is a place where friends and family spend hours passing time, enjoying each other's company, having chats, debating and laughing.

To maintain a garden is work. But it gives great joy and pleasure. I have learned much through gardening. We need to be patient and care for plants if they are to grow. It is the same with humans. We need care and love to grow and develop. I love the statement from the Greek philosopher Socrates who said, *"All people are born to flourish."* Like the world of plants and flowers, we humans are very colourful, delicate and precious but we need to be cared for in the right environment in order to grow and develop.

The garden has allowed me to accept things as they are. I cannot change the shape or colour of the plants or flowers but I can appreciate their differences. I too have to learn to accept myself as 'I am': my colour, my shape, my experience. Sometimes we are in danger of spending too much time and energy changing and denying what is a fact. We often try to force situations into how we would like them. When I can't accept myself as 'I am', I create more tension and stress for myself which in itself prevents positive change taking place. Before any of us can change, we have to accept ourselves, as we are in the present. This does not mean we should stop striving to improve our abilities, talents, imagination or creativity. It just means that we accept things as they are. When we have a clear picture and an awareness of ourselves and our surroundings, change will occur naturally.

Now 'I am' a gardener. My garden is no longer full of trees planted by another, but a place of adventure and fun. It is a living garden offering much to those who sit, watch and listen.

## The Forces of Nature

The waves come and go
Crashing into the landscape.
Their sound touches the soul
Like the harmony of a drum stick
Beating oilskin.

Destruction
Created,
The landscape changes
With the flowing stream
Cascading across the land.

Cool water
Rises,
Meets hot air
Creating mighty winds.
Powerful.

Invisible.
No army
Or man
Can stop
Its mighty force.

Might
From a gentle
Flow,
Wiping out
All in its path.

Yet after the storm
Comes the
Calm.
The beauty of nature
Can be seen again.

Birds dance to the gentle wind,
Fish swim in the powerful sea,
Plants and animals share the same space.
Beauty and colour can only be
Admired.

The changing landscape:
Its beauty,
Its power
Is the only constant
In this changing world.

# 6. The Old Monk and the Garden

*"Is féidir linn"* meaning *"Yes we can"*
— U.S. President Barack Obama, Dublin 2011.

There is a story told of a wise old monk who was doing his daily chores around the garden. Student monks would often gather to watch him work, listen to his wisdom and enjoy the beauty he created with his hands. The wise monk would explain to them how the flowers were fertilised by the insects. He explained that the winds would scatter the new seeds, giving them a greater chance of survival. The monk explained that if a new seed was left in one place it could be in danger of being eaten or destroyed by winds, fire or drought. One of the young monks turned to the old monk and asked, *"If you had one week to live what would you do?"* The wise old monk responded, *"Continue with my garden work."*

There are times in my life when I feel just like the monk. I have much to be grateful for, whether teaching, reading, researching or working in counselling with clients.

This is the garden of my life. Each day I mix with many people. Some are very positive. They give energy and life. Others are so negative that they sap all of my energy. They are like the weeds choking the flowers. I have learned not to spend so much time in the company of those who want to choke the goodness of life. Like the wise monk I need to continue to work with people despite some being difficult. But I continue embracing each day as a new day. I have learned through the journey of life to empower those who want to be in my presence. It is my choice to be with them and their choice to be with me.

Jesus drew a parallel with the planting of seeds. Some seeds fell on good soil and some fell on bad soil, producing weeds and crops. I never understood the value of weeds, yet they continue to be. It is not for me to question why the Creator allows weeds to continue to grow and do so much damage. It looks like they are part of the Divine plan.

If I carry hatred in my heart or curse those who offend me, then I become like a gardener planting weeds, constantly creating pain and hardship for myself.

The sooner I can let go of anger, jealousy, hatred, bitterness and resentment, the sooner I will grow and flourish as a human being. Then I will discover who 'I am'. We all need to be patient with ourselves.

One day I watched my son trying to help a butterfly emerge from its chrysalis by breaking it open. He did not succeed. I explained to him this is a stage of growth often referred to as a pupa, where the body of the caterpillar is transforming into an adult butterfly. This process could take about ten to fourteen days as a chrysalis, then the butterfly is ready to emerge. The butterfly will emerge in its own time; only patience is required.

I invite you to continue practising patience, beginning by being patient with yourself. We all need to ask why we rush through some moments just to get to the next moment?

Treasure each moment, embrace the moment and accept the moment for what it is. In time the moment will reveal its beauty like the butterfly. All things will emerge in their own time. Don't rush them. Open your heart and be free of bitterness and anger. Try to be non-judgmental with yourself and those around you. How do you care for your garden? Spend time nurturing love, kindness, forgiveness, generosity, patience and wisdom while living in the present moment.

## The Beauty of Stars

Bright and beautiful,
Shining in the dark.
Giving compass
To ships at night.

Too many to be counted,
Too many to be explored,
Each a million miles away,
Circled by its own galaxy.

Each star will come and go.
Time passes,
Yet its uniqueness
Will be replaced by another.

In the eyes of a child
The star will shine,
Bright like a loved one
Gone from this world.

To Eternity.
Creating
New star
Divinity.

*Walking On Air* by Francis O' Toole

# 7. Adversity and Acceptance

*"People have a hard time letting go of their suffering.
Out of a fear of the unknown, they prefer suffering that
is familiar."* — Thich Nhat Hanh.

In 1982 I entered the seminary in Thurles, Co Tipperary,
(now MIC, St. Patrick's College) at the age of 17. Still a
child but wanting to become a man. For me, the transition
from secondary school to seminary life was not so difficult. I
came from a good Catholic home where Catholic values
were given high priority. The daily rosary was said as a
family and I often went to Mass daily, especially during
religious calendar events like Advent and Lent. At school
my days were influenced by the Christian brothers who
emphasised both prayer and study in our daily life. Mind
you, I was not a highly-motivated student in school. I
would have preferred to be with friends and playing sports
than studying.

In fifth year in secondary school I got an opportunity to go
Lourdes in the south of France with a large group of
young people and priests from the diocese. This was a
religious pilgrimage and it was here at the age of 16 that I
decided to become a priest. People often talk about the
"call" to religious life…well, here I found my call. I was
fascinated by the thousands who gathered in Lourdes to
pray, I was fascinated by the thousands of sick people who
gathered in the hope of a miracle. For me, the real miracle
of Lourdes was the thousands of people who found peace
of mind as they sat in silence or in prayer at the grotto to
Our Lady. This was the first of many of my trips to

Lourdes; later as a priest I went with pilgrims and worked as a volunteer with the sick.

I was reminded here of a passage from scripture where Jesus cures a crippled woman on the Sabbath day. When Jesus saw the woman, who was possessed by a spirit for eighteen years, she was bent double and unable to stand up. He called her over to him and said, *"Woman, you are rid of your infirmity"* and he laid his hands on her (Luke 13:10–17). Further, he called his accusers *"hypocrites"* and challenged their hypocrisy. Jesus leads by example by standing with those who need help, especially the sick and those alienated from society for whatever reason.

I felt I had a call to care for those who experienced pain and darkness. Somewhere I wanted to be a companion to the sick, I wanted to enter into their darkness and journey with them at least part of the way along their lonely and frightening road. Seminary life was allowing me to find the answer to this call. There were times when I was lonely, afraid and so unsure. I entered the seminary with a very simple faith. I often think this was complicated by the many dogmatic teachings and canon law of the church which was slowly revealed to me over the next six years.

I had hope and belief in the gospel and its message. As a priest, I wanted to follow in the footsteps of Jesus and to preach about his message of love. I worked in active ministry for ten years. I got involved in the lives of people and shared in their pain, sickness and death. I practised listening to the cries of people and I tried to empathise with their pain, which I found really difficult at times. At times I found myself helpless, because I could not take their pain away. I wanted to treat all people as equal and wanted them to know I was there for them to help in their struggle and to celebrate in their good times. I wanted to meet each person as an equal and allow them to recognise that I cared for them and would not run away. There were times when this was difficult. There were times when I was uncertain in my work or unsure in the direction I should take. On many occasions I was there when people experienced brokenness because of the pains of life, either the death of a child or sickness or brokenness in relationships. There were times when I wanted to run away from it all. Yet deep within I wanted to be there working with those who were broken; I know they could not avoid their pain and yet alongside this wish to run, despite my human feelings, is a real love to support those who were broken.

I have often said to people by way of reassurance that it is okay to cry, that tears have a healing power insofar as they show pain and let it out in tears of release. I believe it's important to give people permission to cry because when the tears are past, the person generally feels better and comforted.

Then I discovered that I can only care for others when I first recognised the brokenness within myself. I believe that to be a caring person one does not have to have all the answers or solutions and this may mean accepting that *we have limited power*. I think we need to be stripped of our titles. I need to be aware of my own limitations and my own identity in order to be fully present to others, to support others, just be there as a human being with no labels or roles. For example, I am not the priest or teacher. I am another human being on a journey through life and, at this moment in time, I am willing to stay with those in pain who need support. As a priest this was not always easy to do, especially if the other person had a different value system or beliefs.

31

But the greatest lesson I learned in the priesthood was that when I could accept others and myself as I am, then I will be able to grow. I learned for myself over time that I needed to care more and more for myself in order to be of help to others. I think it has been through acknowledging my own pain and being humbled by the pain in others that I discovered the importance of taking personal care of myself. I now find it important to go for walks, meet friends and read as a way of relaxing. This has helped me to have more energy, especially when caring for others. By recognising my own personal struggle and pain, this has given me a better understanding of 'caring' and it has allowed me as the 'wounded healer' to be more sensitive and compassionate. It is only when we have loved and helped ourselves can we truly reach out in love and help others. I have learned that working in any caring profession, you need to constantly look after your emotional needs and be vigilant in times of loneliness, which is helped by recreation and friendship.

Jean Vanier in his book *'The Broken Body'* reflects on his work with the L'Arche communities, where he shares life with those who have been rejected because they have some kind of disability. Vanier speaks of the pain in these people's lives. Brokenness for me is part of the human experience. Vanier speaks about personal suffering, which should not be ignored or feared: *"So, do not shrink from suffering, but enter into it and discover there the mystery of the presence of Jesus."* I have found 'staying with' my own personal suffering is an awakening experience. It is not an easy road because at times I experience anger, setbacks and doubts. This experience has allowed me to be able to empathise with broken people and it has allowed me to know and understand myself better, especially when others 'press my buttons' and trigger self-doubt. I admit that it takes courage to acknowledge one's own weakness but I agree with Vanier's claim that is only then that we reach 'wholeness'.

This ability to acknowledge our own weakness is a gift from God and it is only through God's unfolding plan that we can help others in their own brokenness. Pain, suffering and rejection are part and parcel of human experience, and when accepted and integrated into our whole life they become part of the road upon which the journey of life is made.

*Walking On Air* by Francis O' Toole

# 8. Lack of Knowledge

*"You can never cross the ocean unless you have the courage to lose sight of the shore."*
— Christopher Columbus.

As part of our formation in the seminary, we had daily prayer, class and study. We were isolated from the outside world. Bells rang at 6:30am for public prayer, followed by private prayer, then the celebration of the Eucharist. We were ready for breakfast at 8:30am. This was followed by lectures for six hours in Philosophy and Theology. Then it was out to the hurling or football field until 4:30pm, a time to get rid of frustration. This was my way of life for six years. The sports field was the only place where I could be free of the institutional rules. Here passion, fists and bad language would emerge.

I was playing football one week before the summer holidays of my third year. After a tackle with an American student, a loud crack was heard as we fell to the ground. My friend seemed to be in pain. When we got to our feet, my friend continued to play on. I had to walk off. I was in shock and in pain. When I got to the sideline, I collapsed. I was told in hospital later that I had a very bad fracture and would spend sixteen weeks in plaster from toe to hip…what a long summer that was going to be!

Seminary life had its challenges and pressures. There was the fun of being on a journey with 130 students with a common focus and a common goal. Many young men entered seminaries after Pope John Paul II's visit to Ireland in 1979. Most of us were ignorant of the issues people were experiencing in the outside world. Bob Geldof was fighting for world aid to feed the hungry and AIDS was killing thousands daily. Meanwhile, we remained behind closed doors in study and prayer. We had half an hour at night to watch the news before night prayer. Then followed silence as we headed to our bedrooms. These contained a small single bed, a desk and a chair for study, and a hand basin. It was strange to think after six years of sheltered life that we were expected to go into the local community as leaders. We were far from ready for the many experiences we would encounter in priestly ministry.

In the seminary we were never encouraged to ask questions. In fact, it was seen as questioning authority. I married after I left the priesthood; the first thing I taught my children was to develop an ability to ask questions, always seek the truth, stick with the facts and research what they could before making any decisions or assumptions.

# 9. Sexual Abuse

*"Survivors of abuse show us the strength of their
personal spirit every time they smile."*
— Jeanne McElvaney.

The darkest days in seminary life were when one of those
I trusted brought me unbearable pain, hurt and destruction
when he sexually abused me. He was a professor priest
and I was a vulnerable student who trusted in his spiritual
guidance, only to be betrayed. Sexual abuse is when you
say *"no"* to sexual contact and the dominant person forces
themselves on you against your will to perform sexual
acts. The abuse is well planned and organised. For me, it
was the person to whom I looked up and even saw as a
role model. The experience would have a profound impact
on my life. I was a young man taking on a life of celibacy,
emotionally confused, damaged by the act of an abuser.

At the time I reported my experience to my spiritual
director. He listened carefully to everything I told him and
wanted all the details. When I was finished revealing my
deepest hurt and pain, he told me to pray for the professor
priest, that he needed forgiveness and strength to continue
with his work. I was thinking my spiritual director cared
about me. This spiritual director inflicted more confusion
and punishment on my life by remaining silent as an
authority figure and requesting I would do likewise. Many
years later I revealed the same story to the Archbishop,
and again words fell on deaf ears. Protection of the good
name of the institution of the church was more important
than my vulnerability.

I was living in my own darkness, lonely and frightened. I now distrust double standards, those who know about abuse but will not do anything. When someone will not listen to your hurt and pain or when they don't want to believe you, they add to your hurt and pain immeasurably.

I worked with Accord for ten years which is predominantly a lay organisation of counsellors working primarily to help people who are experiencing stress in relationships. Thanks to Accord, I trained and worked as a counsellor. Within the church, here was an organisation with its own code of ethics and practice. My experience with Accord has been challenging and allowed me the opportunity to grow personally. It also challenged me as a family therapist to have vision and hope while working with individuals or in relationship counselling. It was here that I first embarked on a journey of self-discovery dealing with my sexual abuse.

I learned that those who suffer sexual abuse need real support, including me. Any kind of abuse is wicked but I think sexual abuse is exceptionally destructive because it is twisted mixture of sexual, physical, emotional, psychological and even spiritual abuse all in one. As a newly-trained therapist, I realised that many people don't want to talk about their abuse. It was the same with me for a long time. I experienced irrational thinking; I wanted to keep it to myself. There was shame. There was anger. There was guilt. There was despair.

Most people get stuck here and are unable to move on. I wonder is it because of the fear nobody will listen? That was my experience.

Sexual abuse can happen anywhere and to anyone. Statistics are staggeringly high when it comes to sexual abuse; one in every three girls and one in every six boys have experienced sexual abuse. The statistics are also very high for adults, especially women. It is not for nothing that Colm O'Gorman named the advocacy organisation for survivors of sexual abuse 'One in Four'.

The fear is that the numbers are far greater because so many cases go unreported. Many victims fear that no one will believe them. It is also a sad reality, especially in the Irish legal system, that many cases will not go to court and of those that do, only a small percentage have a success rate.

It is important to accept that the abuser can be either male or female. He or she is not typically a stranger and in most cases it is a friend, family member or someone known to the victim. It is also normal for the victim to have feelings for the perpetrator, whom they think is caring for them. Regardless of whether or not the abuser is known to the victim, the effect of sexual abuse is lifelong.

It is so important for every abused person to know that they are not to blame. They need to know that the abuser is in a very powerful position and that sexual abuse is not their fault.

I have found that the best way of dealing with sexual abuse is to talk about it. If we learn to talk about it, then a process of healing will take place.

I have learned ways of dealing with my own personal conflict and sexual abuse. Firstly I must accept myself as I am and be non-judgemental. Feelings are neither right nor wrong. Naming my fears and concerns have gone a long way towards taming them for me. I also recognise the necessity for personal counselling. Each counselling session and each interaction with another human being brings something to the surface in me. I cannot deal with abuse on my own but need to talk to others about it.

I also developed coping skills that I need to change. I tended to avoid what had happened. But now I know I cannot heal if I am avoiding the problem.

I often made excuses for the person who abused me. I would say he had a drink problem or he was lonely or he did not intend to hurt me. I was taking the responsibility away from the abuser. This denied me my feelings of hurt and pain. So I stopped making excuses for the abuser.

I also minimised the experience. I tried to pretend it was a small part of my life, it was no big deal. This is a way of coping but now, thirty-three years later, I acknowledge this was a serious abuse and I denied myself when I minimised it.

I also need to work on denial. For too long I denied that I was abused. Once again the abuser was free but I was caught in my own self-created prison. I am very aware that I need to continue to work on myself, my own beliefs, fears, misconceptions and unanswered questions. I need to believe that others do care for and love me.

This recognition gives me certain freedom and also gives me hope. I have practised mindfulness, enabling me to have greater self knowledge and self-awareness, and this will hopefully lead me to greater freedom, acceptance and not a judgemental attitude of self.

If you have been abused and haven't told anybody, my first recommendation is to talk to someone: a friend or a professional counsellor.

If somebody discloses an abuse to you. I suggest being calm and being aware that the disclosure is really difficult for the other person. Do not judge the person. Listen to everything they have to say. Do not react or show any signs of disbelief, disgust or anger. Advise that person to seek professional help. Always remember if the person is a minor (under 18 years of age in Ireland), you have a duty to report this to the professional authorities. The time has come when no institution or church member should be protected by government if they are inflicting pain on the most vulnerable in society.

*Walking On Air* by Francis O' Toole

# 10. Where Is God?

*"When I stand before God at the end of my life, I would hope that I would not have a single bit of talent left and could say, 'I used everything you gave me.'"*
— Erma Bombeck.

As a student of Theology, I was very fortunate to get the opportunity to work in Rome for a short period. At that time I was fascinated by history. In Rome I could turn any street corner, look at an old building and there in front of my eyes history would unfold. From Roman times to world wars, Rome can tell a story. Yet when I looked beyond the walls and ruins of past splendours, I couldn't help but feel the pain and the human cost of history. Much of the Vatican treasure — gold, priceless artefacts — was plundered from places like Haiti, Cuba and Mexico. The Catholic church has been collecting such wealth for 2,000 years. This is far from the gospel of Jesus, the founder of Christianity. He lived and worked with the poor. Today the Catholic church is the wealthiest institution on earth. So much was achieved by different cultural groups and yet so much of it was created out of human pain, suffering and destruction.

During my stay in Rome, a friend who worked in Vatican City got permission for me to visit the inside of the Holy Walls of the Vatican. I was so excited that day crossing the square of St. Peter's Basilica knowing that I had permission to pass the Swiss guard. The Pontifical Swiss guard is a small military force who are responsible for the safety of the Pope and the security of the Apostolic palace. This army was established in 1506 by Pope Julius II. Here, more history revealed itself in public and private treasures, the hidden wealth of the Roman Catholic Church. I even stood at the window where the Popes greeted and blessed millions who gathered to pray over the centuries. Nevertheless, in my search for God, he wasn't visible in this magnificent place of wealth, history and splendour.

I found it hard to feel God's presence even in the awe-inspiring building of St. Peter's. I went into one of the side chapels where the faithful gathered so that I could pray away from the noisy tourists flashing their cameras and pointing to the next stop on their guides. As I prayed, I could smell the candles burning and see those around me paying homage to their God. Then, in the stillness, I felt a moment of grace. Sitting in a quiet corner of St. Peter's, I could sense the presence of God. I stopped looking outwards at the activity around me. I stopped searching. Here in the silence of my heart was God's presence. He was with me all the time. He was with me on my journey. He was with me while I was searching. He was with me walking, sleeping and in prayer.

There is a beautiful psalm in the Old Testament: Psalm 139. It tells of how God knows us from the beginning to the end of our journey of life. He knows our every thought and breath.

I find it difficult to meditate and pray daily. Yet I want to converse with the Creator of the universe, the "'I am', the Way, the Truth and the Life" (John 14:6). That same day in St. Peter's, I went to the celebration of Mass to listen and feel the presence of God. This presence could be felt in the words of scripture, in the priest celebrating the

Mass, in the Eucharist and in the people gathered. Create the change, say yes to 'I am'. This will allow you to experience the presence of God in your daily life. You will find this presence not only in sacred places like a church but in every moment of your life, within nature and with the people you love.

*Walking On Air* by Francis O' Toole

# 11. Living the Message

*"You'll never find peace of mind until you listen to your heart."* — George Michael.

When I was ordained a deacon in 1987 it was part of my formation to work in a parish in London. I was entrusted to the care of an old parish priest who had a major alcohol problem; one drink was too much and a million wasn't enough. Yet this man was dearly loved by his parishioners because of his kindness and wisdom. He was with them throughout the years to celebrate their good times, baptisms, weddings, parish occasions. He was also there to listen to their pain and empathise with their suffering in times of trouble.

One lunchtime he asked me to go down to Hyde Park and preach the gospel in public. My heart sank at the thought and I was petrified. How I could preach the gospel without the security of the pulpit? But eventually I trusted that I would be guided by the Holy Spirit to do the right thing. Surely if I was committed to following Christ I could go and preach the gospel. When I got to Hyde Park I cringed with embarrassment and fear and I knew that I wouldn't be able to carry out the task. When I reached my destination I was relieved to see that there were very few people around. I could see a few drunks so I went and chatted to them. Then I had a brainwave: I would volunteer to do the soup-runs at night helping the outcast, homeless and those who had given up on life. I did do the soup-runs and it was a profoundly humbling exercise.

At the end of the summer I told the parish priest about my experience in failing to preach the gospel. He replied, *"Yes, but you will be rewarded for living it."* A good leader brings out the best in other people and empowers them to believe in themselves and to appreciate their skills, talents and abilities. My parish priest was certainly a good leader.

Our society needs leaders who give hope to others, who will inspire others to follow in their footsteps. The world is broken and full of pain. In July 2016 Pope Francis said, *"The world is at war"* and he elaborated by saying that it is *"...not a war of religion. This is a war of interests. There is a war of money. There is a war for natural resources. There is a war for domination of peoples. This is a war."*

Ask yourself if you can become a leader to fight in this war. It could be connected to money, migration, wars, peace or poverty. We need leaders who will inspire others to follow a path of justice, truth, love, appreciation of the earth, science and arts. We need more leaders in every walk of life. Are you that kind of person: the kind of person who has a real passion and belief that they have a message for the world, be it at a community, national or international level?

## Living

Creativity will bring wealth.
Dance
Will bring joy.

Wisdom
Will bring acceptance.
The just man will be happy.
The universe will shine.

Truth the way,
Love the light.

The soul is free
To dance
With the rhythm of
Life.

*Walking On Air* by Francis O' Toole

# 12. Knowledge and Life

*"We must become the change we want to see."*
— Mahatma Gandhi.

I was ordained a priest in 1988 after six years of study in St. Patricks College, Thurles, County Tipperary. I knew within my soul there was a mission to change the world. I had high expectations and zeal within. For me the time was right. Yet at the age of twenty-three, how much real experience did I have? What did I know about the world I was going to encounter? I knew that as a priest I would encounter many challenging situations, great moments and sad occasions.

In Ireland during the eighties there was a great welcome for the priest in the local community. It was also a time of high unemployment and emigration.

I listened to the young ordained men who came back to the seminary to share their experiences of being on the missions. They talked about the missions with great pride and their love for the daily work. On hearing these experiences I felt my blood boiling. There was fire in my belly. I felt ready to go out and change the world. I felt that I had a 'mission'.

On the day of my ordination the sun shone brightly. Family, friends and people from my home community all came to celebrate a wonderful occasion. Thirty-two men were to be ordained to the priesthood and five from the town of Templemore, where I hailed from. To be ordained a priest was to be thrust into a life of celibacy and obedience to the bishop, and sent on a mission to preach and teach the gospel. This mission is best summed up in the words of the prophet Micah: "*to act justly, to love tenderly and to walk humbly with your God.*" (Micah 6:8)

The first pastoral appointment on which I was sent was based in Knocklong, County Limerick. This parish has a small population with two churches and two schools. One church is based in Knocklong and the other Glenbrohane; it was built before the famine. It is set along the northern slopes of the Sliabh Riagh — Sliabh Rí — The Hill of the King. I was told by the parishioners that the army of Cormac Mac Airt, High King of Ireland, was defeated in the area. Today you will find a stone circle on the hilltop. A group of stones called 'The King's Chair' can be seen.

I could see the wisdom of building a church in such a remote place, amongst the beauty of the mountain with a panoramic view of lustrous green fields, trees and rivers. This place gave me a glimpse of heaven's beauty. The church bells rang and the people gathered from far and near to pray and celebrate. They would also give thanks for the richness of their harvest. Here I experienced not only a deep religious faith but also a deep Celtic spirituality rooted in the generations who gathered in this little church.

During the three months I spent here, I set up a folk group and summer camp for young people. What I really enjoyed about this community was their ability to do the ordinary things of life in an extraordinary way.

It seems that the Archbishop of Cashel and Emly was content in his belief that I had the ability to settle into country life. I came from a rural town, a family of fourteen: three sisters and ten brothers. I had spent six years in the seminary and never stayed in a house on my own at any stage of my life. The reality of the demands of celibacy hit me like a ton of bricks. Having to live as a celibate was a real struggle. No matter how I filled my day, it was never easy coming back to an empty house. No one to talk to, no one to share feelings with, no intimacy. Looking back, I think this was an unrealistic expectation to impose on a young man.

I was always fortunate to be surrounded by people and friends who cared, shared and gave support when needed. My priestly journey continued from Knocklong to a new parish in South Tipperary: Annacarty and Donohill. Before my appointment I didn't even know such a place existed. This was a rural community with a population of fifteen hundred people, three primary schools and two churches. In the village where I resided, Annacarty, there was a church, a pub/shop and a GAA field. The first day I arrived I felt a little disillusioned. I questioned myself about my mission to change the world.

Before I knew it, I was stuck into the work, visiting the sick and teaching in the local VEC school in the parish of Cappawhite. I was greeted warmly in the homes of the community. I became a part of every family, despite not having any family. The community spirit was positive, caring and supportive with strong bonds evident on and off the GAA field. We were trained in the seminary to rise early with prayer in our hearts and a plan for our day. In the seminary this was easy because everything was organised for us. All we had to do was to respond to the sound of the bell, just like Pavlov's dog. It was in the 1890s that a Russian physiologist Ivan Pavlov discovered salivation in dogs in response to being fed: he would ring a bell, the dogs entered the room looking for their food. Even though it was my choice to be there, we were conditioned to think and feel in a certain way. All of our studies were academic; we were trained to think from the chin up but from the neck down did not exist. Our emotions, feelings and sexuality was never discussed as part of our formation to priestly life.

But really, my life was simple, easy, non-threatening and rewarding as I got to know the people. I would awake at cock-crow, have breakfast, say my breviary, take a walk to the local church and watch the cows as they lined up to head to the milking parlour. I watched the sheep and the horses; all of this beauty in front of my eyes before I got to the church to celebrate Mass. Sunday was a busy day at Mass with full attendance. But during the week I was lucky to have between three and ten parishioners.

After Mass, I planned my day with ease and happiness. I always had the ability to enjoy the moment, a skill I developed through the calmness of morning prayer and meditation. I wanted to be totally available when the phone rang or when a parishioner came knocking on my door looking for a kind smile and compassion. For me, this was the life of a priest: to live in the moment and to be available for the parishioners when their need arose. It was a simple way to live with no major questions about life and free from financial pressure or family commitments. Somehow I was transformed from a person with a mission to change the world into a person with a vision to change myself, to adapt, adjust and fit into country life. I accepted that I needed to do my duty. But there was also a part of me frustrated and annoyed with the Bishop who was my boss. I was 23 years of age, full of energy and life, full of high ideals and vision about ministry, believing I was not given an opportunity to do something greater.

# 13. Country Life

*"The future belongs to those who believe in the beauty of their dreams."* — Eleanor Roosevelt.

During this time, the late eighties, conflict existed in every day Ireland with high unemployment, emigration and poverty. Killings were witnessed daily on the streets of Northern Ireland; killings in the name of religion. Church scandals began to creep in. Allegations of sexual abuse of children associated with Catholic institutions and clerics in several countries started to receive wide publicity. The authority church led by Catholic bishops remained silent. I found this really difficult to accept. It caused me deep pain to think there were people using their clerical status to really hurt and injure children. There were times when I wore the black suit and white collar in shame, knowing that some clerics brought such evil into the church.

On an international level wars in Afghanistan and Iraq were looming. Global warming was discussed. AIDS was the new disease killing millions. There were false prophets talking about the end of the world in 2000. This list could be extended. But in Annacarty and Donohill, the big news in the schoolyard, the GAA grounds, shops and pubs was the weather forecast. Everyone in the village knew when it was going to rain and when the sun would shine. It took me a while to get my head around this obsession. Then I realised the weather could directly affect the parishioners' lives. As a priest in the community, I too became a specialist on the weather, offering prayers from the pulpit for fine weather.

I also used the pulpit on Sundays to give sermons. I used to spend ages preparing. I even practised giving a sermon at home in the silence of my house. There were times I could get it so wrong. I will always remember the day news broke about Bishop Eamonn Casey fathering a son. I only heard part of the morning RTÉ news where they talked all about his achievements as a bishop; I presumed he'd died. In my morning homily, I used his life story as example to us, a role model, especially the way he reached out to the Irish emigrants in England; then I prayed that he may rest in peace. The sacristan handed me a piece of paper telling me he was alive and well and the news of the day was about him fathering a child. I climbed down from the pulpit with a big red face. Only afterwards did I laugh out loud when a parishioner said *"It could happen to a bishop"*. This same pulpit was often used by others to preach about fire and brimstone, putting the fear of God into people. Thankfully, I left the seminary preaching about a loving God who cares for His people. I walked their fields and happily prayed for fine weather and blessed their animals.

At lunch time I'd come back to the house to the smell of food prepared by the part-time housekeeper. What a luxury for a young man! In some way the housekeeper was trying to create the feeling of normality within this empty house. I'd listen to the answering machine, then read the national paper to see what was happening in the world. I always finished with the local papers and newsletters to find out what was happening on the GAA field, who won at bingo and what was happening in the youth club. The housekeeper could fill in the gaps with the local news!

Sadly, during my time there I encountered many tragedies, farm accidents and car accidents. I was burying the old and the young. There was a lovely tradition in this community where the bereaved family asked a friend or neighbour to dig the grave for the family member who died. It was seen as a great honour to be asked then during the day friends and family called for a chat and offered some refreshments, usually a bottle of whiskey and some sandwiches. These events brought the community to a standstill. I was never comfortable as the leading celebrant of a funeral. There was never a right time to die; there were always loved ones left behind dealing with loss, grief and death. I found it really difficult to stand up and try to say the right words to help a grieving family. What do I say to a mum who has lost her son to suicide or to a wife and mother of young children who lost her husband to cancer? I would write and rewrite the homily several times. In the end I entrusted myself to God's hands to help me say the right words of comfort and explain how our faith can be a consolation in times of grief. This was always difficult. But I too was affected by the grief that other people experience. I will always remember the day I was called out to a farm tragedy where a young man died; he was a close personal friend. I was in shock. Even though I was struggling with my own grief and unanswered questions, duty called me to abandon my own feelings and be strong for others. I found this so difficult. There was no time or space to share my grief. As tears flowed the community offered support in every way possible. These people knew how to empathise with each other. The support and strength of the community was most evident during a tragedy. The news would be on the lips of every person for weeks. The next GAA game or parish function distracted from the sadness and allow us to move on.

I often sat in the hills of Annacarty at the top of the parish to be alone, sensing the stillness and allowing myself space to catch my breath. I would look across the beauty of the landscape, listen to the singing of the birds or watch the flowing rivers cascading from the hilltop. Sometimes I would just lie down on the grass, smell the air and watch the clouds forming and reforming in the skies above.

At home I continued to pray and meditate, a practice encouraged in the seminary. This enabled us to be still in chaos and place ourselves in the presence of the Lord. It became the rock to fall back on in difficult times. There was always the question about what to do next. In fact, there were many times when I would question my ability and purpose. I often asked the question, *"What is it all about?"* but failed to come up with an answer. At moments like this I would say, *"Be calm and carry on."* When I was experiencing self doubt friends and parishioners, whether aware of it or not, would carry me through those moments. Ar scáth a chéile a mhaireann na daoine. It is in the shelter of each other that people survive. I realised that the parish community was okay, with or without me. They were a stable, caring, understanding and spiritual people before I came on the scene. In fact, they taught me more about life than I ever discovered on my own.

It was here, thanks to the Principal of the local VEC school, that I developed my love for computers. In the late eighties very few homes in Ireland had computers. I was one of the first priests in the diocese with a personal computer. Despite being isolated in a country parish, I knew that with the press of a button and a good DSL line (weather permitting) that the world would come and meet me. I could connect to a bigger world, learn new things, hear about progress or lack of progress in wars. I could get different philosophical views. The best luxury was the ability to receive emails worldwide. I could plan long-distance trips and even cancel them.

For me this became a new mission: to work on computers and learn as much as possible. It was like I could enter the biggest library in the world without leaving the comfort of my home. If I was to have more answers to unsolved questions, I needed to know about the world. For me this was a new way of finding the answers to philosophical questions, like: "Why do bad things happen to good people?" I always knew that we need to question the world in which we live. It's important at least to ask the questions, even though we may not always find the answers. Bringing the world wide web into the sitting room allowed me to connect with the bigger world and the local community. I knew that having knowledge of both would enrich my journey and those I walked with.

I could smell the grass, watch farming life in action, awake with the rising sun, and at the end of the day reflect on all the experiences while watching the setting sun and waiting for the bright stars to light up the sky. Each day brought me new challenges, joys and awakenings. These experiences made me into the person I am.

The lives and stories of the people I witnessed allowed me to discover the richness of the world. This richness was not in the dreams of people looking outwards, but was found deep within their hearts where vision was stirred with passion: by their ability to do ordinary things extraordinarily well, empathise, live in the moment, smile and talk. There was always a helping hand. I discovered their spirituality was greater than my faith.

What I loved about this community was that there was always time for talk. The local doctor greeted his patients with a smile and talked about the weather before listening to their story. The farmer would stop his work to talk to those passing, the shopkeeper had time for everyone, and the publican was like a secret confessor listening patiently to stories repeated night after night. There would always be a gathering of people at the church gate before and after Mass. I often wondered if this was a time to share parish news or was it a time when some farmers would meet to make a sale on a bullock! At this time I was elected chairperson of the local GAA club Éire Óg; members of this club had great pride in their history. The real bonus for me was a guaranteed ticket to the All-Ireland hurling final: these tickets were like gold dust. The parishioners were very proud of one of their own Pat Fox who was on the successful county team that was to bring the Liam MacCarthy Cup back to Tipperary. I have to say this brought great joy into the local community. It gave us nights of celebrations in the local pub and many a baby was baptised and photographed with this famous cup.

I often asked myself if I could connect and learn about the world of technology using www while at the same time connect to the local community? Is it like living in two different worlds in one day? As we have found in the present era of the smartphone, so many of us are constantly distracted by social media and the internet is increasingly allowing the virtual world become part of the real world. But I know I was not lonely or empty. Each day I was learning something new about life. I now realise that the real mission is not about changing the world. The real journey is from the head to the heart. My mission is to change myself.

# 14. The Undertaker

*"The life of the dead is placed in the memory of the living."* — Marcus Tullius Cicero.

I recall one winter's night sitting by the fire reading a book when the door bell rang…I felt my stomach drop. It was after midnight and I knew the person at the door would be the bearer of bad news. I answered; I spoke with the person whose brother had passed away. He wanted me to go to their home to give the last rites to his brother. I told him I would follow after I got ready. I then phoned the undertaker to inform him of the death and asked if he would give me a lift to the house of the deceased as I didn't know where the man lived.

I got into the hearse that smelled oddly of pollen from flowers and listened to the buzz of a fly who had managed to sneak its way onto the dashboard. We drove for a few miles up into the hills of Annacarty, passing Ballysheedy Castle, the oldest building in the parish; this was the O'Dwyer stronghold until the Cromwellian Plantation in the 1650s. It is said that there is an underground tunnel connecting the castle to a nearby monastic settlement in Kilnamanagh. When we arrived at the cottage, we had to climb a gate and walk across a field to get to the house. I was led into a small bedroom. The room was dull, showing no evidence of the man's personality. There were no pictures on the wall, no books on the dresser, no clothes flung on an armchair. The only thing that was eye-catching was the rigid body on the neatly-folded bed. His skin had coloured slightly, tainted grey, his body cold and rigid. The doctor spoke, telling me the cause and time of death.

Looking upon his face, I remembered the times I had seen him at church, always in the same seat and saying his prayers with dedication.

After performing the last rites on the man, I helped the undertaker to lift the body into a temporary tin coffin and place it into the hearse. The drive to the funeral home was long and silent. Neither the undertaker nor I made conversation and I found myself feeling uneasy as I could hear the buzz from that misguided fly who was still in the hearse.

About ten miles out, I could hear noises from the back of the hearse. An unsettling scratching noise. I tried to ignore it, thinking I was being paranoid and imagining things, and I turned my attention back to the road.

The scratching noise began to get louder and louder until I couldn't ignore it. I looked at the undertaker and I noticed the same uneasiness I felt was shown across his face. Stopping the hearse we opened the back door and looked at the image of the haunting casket. We lifted it out onto the road and began to unclip the clips holding down the lid. With unspoken mutual agreement we lifted up the lid and were scared as something jumped up at us screeching. I found myself looking into a pair of emerald green eyes with spiked black hair and frightened. *"A cat"* is all the undertaker said in a monotone voice and a shocked expression across his face. For a moment we just stood there, listening to the sound of our pounding hearts and watching as the cat ran away. Gracefully and respectfully we placed the coffin back into the hearse. We then sat at the side of the road, still in shock. I heard laughter. It was coming from the undertaker and then from me, it was the sound of relief. We continued on our journey and talked about our experience until we got to the funeral home.

## The Farmer

The farmer ponders
Seeds in hand;
Soil is rich
Ready to enrich.

As seeds are planted
Nothing's for granted
Patience demanded
As nature commanded.

With delight
The earth gives life;
With basket in hand
Collects from the land.

The church bells ring;
Time to sing
Praise the Lord
God is King.

Give thanks.
Fruit and veg
Taken from the hedge
Placed on the ledge.

Left to the market,
Awaiting sales target,
Customers come,
Customers go.

With straw hat
A great place for a chat,
Smiles give rise
To bright market eyes.

The farmer
Happy
As goods change hands
With lots of demands.

Returning to his farm
Looking at the barn
He prays
No harm will come to his farm.

# 15. Fighter

*"He who conquers himself is the mightiest warrior."*
— Confucius.

When I was a student in secondary school, I loved taking part in sports: hurling, football, swimming, boxing, soccer, basketball, etc. The one sport in which I excelled was boxing. Whenever someone asked, *"Why boxing?"* I'd jokingly reply, *"I've ten brothers, so I needed to develop the art of self-defence."* My proudest moments were representing my county and province as a boxer in the National Stadium, Dublin. To reach that level I had to train endlessly: run, skip, shadow box. I spent hours punching boxing bags and sparring with members of my club and other clubs. I fought in the All-Ireland Championship against a young man who went on to box for Ireland in the Olympics. When working in the parish of Annacarty, I set up, trained and organised a successful boxing club that ran for five years.

One of the boxing club's highlights was the night newly-crowned world champion Barry McGuigan visited us for a five-minute photo shoot. For the night, I had created a boxing ring from bales of hay and had organised sparring matches between the young lads in the parish hall. Barry was so taken aback by the spirit of the club that he stayed for over two hours, giving his professional advice and posing for photos with each boy and his family.

Every boxing match was tough, painful and psychologically draining. Yet there was a wonderful feeling in being able to stand up for myself, going it alone, taking punches from my opponent and getting up again if an opponent knocked me down. This demanded good, stable mental ability. At the end of each boxing match, the referee would call both boxers to the centre of the ring, await the judge's decision and then raise the winner's hand in the air. If my hand was raised, I would automatically jump for joy, bang my gloves together and hug my opponent despite the pain. I would feel the cobwebs being blown from my mind and my heart purified. The smile of success overcomes any pain.

Boxing taught me how important it is to trust myself. If I trust my ability, I am in touch with my authority and intuition. If I make mistakes, I just need to be thankful that I had an opportunity for learning. It is crucial to trust myself, to honour and respect my feelings and emotions, to be responsible for my decisions and my well-being. I cannot blame others for how I feel, and I need to be responsible and take ownership of my feelings, my thoughts and my emotions.

'I am' a fighter. It's okay to shout for joy when I succeed in life. There is no greater feeling than when my dream becomes a reality, especially after working hard to create that reality for myself. Celebrate success and others will want to join in your success. I encourage you to never give up till the final bell.


## Boxer

Boxer, Boxer,
Boxer in corner,
Glove in hand,
Awaits bell,
Next command.

Battle begins.
No songs are sung,
Blood on cheek,
Sweat on chest,
What a mess.

Boxer in corner,
You are the best,
In need of rest.

Winning glory,
Losing poorly,
That's okay.
Next round
Play surely.

Boxer in corner,
Knock out,
Pull out.
You will fall
But arise
For the prize.

No pain, no gain.
Hand is raised,
Full of praise.

Boxer in corner,
The fight remains the same,
A winning game.

*Walking On Air* by Francis O' Toole

# 16. Holy Well

*"I am rooted, but I flow."* — Virginia Woolf.

In folklore stories told in Ireland about wells and their powers from the 'otherworld', waters flow into our world to fill springs or gush forth as rivers, such as the beautiful Boyne and Shannon. These rivers are linked with the goddesses Boann and Sionann.

The people believed that drinking from holy wells or bathing in them would confer the power of the 'otherworld' as poetic inspiration, wisdom or healing. Salmon or trout, considered supernatural fish, are still thought to appear in a well's depths to those looking for omens for the future.

It's estimated there are approximately 3,000 holy wells in Ireland. The largest is St. Patrick's Well, which is located in a stunning valley close to the village of Marlfield, Clonmel, County Tipperary. Holy wells had both material and spiritual value for our ancestors. They had material value because they provided an unlimited supply of fresh water. Spiritually it was said that holy wells contained magical powers, granted wishes and that by drinking the water, you would be cured of your ailments. Every well had its own power known to the local community, for example the power to heal sore lips, bad eyesight or chronic diseases. Throughout the centuries pilgrims gathered at wells making wishes and offering prayers.

Some of these wells go back hundreds and even thousands of years but they were blessed by the church as a way of getting pagans to believe that the wells were associated with baptism, the water of the Christian life. Legend has it that St. Patrick prayed at Marlfield well while on his journey to Cashel to meet the powerful King Aengus of Munster, whom he converted from paganism and baptised into the Christian Church. Hundreds of people gathered at this ceremony as it symbolised the end of paganism and the beginning of Christianity in Munster. During the ceremony, it is said that St. Patrick thrust his crozier into the foot of the king who remained silent as he thought it was all part of the baptismal ritual! While a possible disaster was averted for St. Patrick, it was the beginning of Christianity on the famous Rock of Cashel. This ancient site became the castle for many a king of Munster, including the famous Brian Boru, and later it became one of the major key Christian centres of medieval Ireland. The next time you are in Tipperary, allow time to visit this awesome historical site, go to the visitor centre where you will hear many a story like the one above about St. Patrick.

Like many religions, the Christian church continues to choose water as a sacramental because it is so necessary for life. It can cleanse, purify, quench thirst. It is needed for growth of the harvest and so much more. In baptism, we believe it washes away all our sins. We need water daily to survive, as do the plant and animal kingdoms.

I have a little pond in my back garden. It is a nice water feature with fish, but the pond also attracts insects, birds and little animals, creating its own world. I have often sat there pondering life and its many mysteries. Some communities have carried on the tradition of making wishes and praying at the holy wells, while others have stopped because the local church has decided that it is not in the best interest of the people.

I invite you to visit St. James' Holy Well, Donohill, County Tipperary. This holy well has its origins in pagan times but was dedicated to St. James in pre-Norman times. It is said to 'have the cure' for sore eyes. Over the years, people would wipe their eyes with a cloth and then place the cloth on a whitethorn bush beside the well to symbolise the leaving of their troubles behind. Every year, on the feast of St James, a special devotion to the saint or a 'pattern' took place in the parish and it centred on the well. The pattern always brought great excitement to the village of Donohill. Tents were set up from which people sold alcohol, among many other things, on the feast day. The debauchery and intemperance at these patterns came to the attention of Archbishop Bray and in 1797 he suppressed *"for all time the holding of such patterns anywhere in the diocese of Cashel and Emly."*

In 1840 when scholar and topographer John O'Donovan surveyed the area, he referenced the holy well, detailing it and the whitethorn bush wearing cloths of all colours. It is also said that O'Sullivan Beare, Prince of Beare, and his companions drank from the well after they battled at the Moate of Donohill. In 1991 while researching the history of the locality, I became fascinated with the stories and history of the St. James Holy Well and I had the well restored with the aid of FÁS and the newly-formed Tipperary Multeen Tourism.

I believe that we need to get in touch with Celtic spirituality, to connect with nature and prayer. Look out for the local holy well in your community, see what insights you gain and maybe your wishes and prayers will be answered. Throw in a little stone or coin and watch the ripple effect. Consider the ripple effect in your own life. Each day your deeds and actions touch the lives of other people and nature. Pray at the

holy well that all your actions will be refreshing and life-
giving for those you love: your family, friends, people
in the community and even your enemies.

## Sleep

Sleep,
Deep in resting,
Doors shut,
Darkness sets in,
The world no more.

My safety is felt,
Warm and glowing,
Comfort of the womb.

The ship afloat,
Rocks on the sea,
Waves beat like a drum.

Heartbeat rhythm
Flows with life,
Eternal.

# 17. Cup of Tea

*"A man may die, nations may rise and fall, but an idea lives on. Ideas have endurance without death."*
— John F. Kennedy.

Memorable moments often happen when least expected. I was out on pastoral duties visiting the local community. Often I found myself in a house with people who were not practising or who had given up their religion. Most of the time I was greeted with kindness and welcome. The Irish never lost the gift of chat and welcome. On one occasion I found myself in the home of a man who clearly stated he was an atheist but still welcomed me into his house. I accepted the invitation; who knows what can happen over a cup of tea?

During our discussion I went on the defensive and stated that one would have to be ignorant or arrogant not to believe in God. I was young, full of passion for my work and unwise. He went on to give me all the reasons and arguments for not believing in God and the reason he gave up on religion. He spoke about man's inhumanity to man. He asked why bad things happen to good people. He spoke about holy wars and crusades because of religion and wealth in churches. In most cases the arguments he gave were based on historical fact and I had no counter-argument. He could prove his facts from countless history books. In the end all I could say was, *"I'm sorry for suggesting that you were ignorant or arrogant."* I told him I believed in religion because I found it a formal way of giving expression to the Creator. I spoke of love, forgiveness, compassion, truth, justice and wisdom. In the end I just said, *"I go to church because it gives me a way to express my feelings of thanksgiving for the gift of life and nature. I also express my weakness and ask the Creator for the strength and courage to live a better life."*

This cup of tea allowed for an expression and sharing of ideas, views and passion. It was a time of sharing and caring. As we parted I asked, *"Is it true that you are a great musician and singer?"* He replied proudly, *"Yes."* I invited my atheist friend to set up a folk group in our church. He replied, *"Yes, see you next Sunday."*

## Uniqueness

Ashes we arise,
Dust we return,
Created equal,
None the same.

# 18. Jump for Joy

*"I learned that courage was not the absence of fear, but the triumph over it. The brave man is not he who does not feel afraid, but he who conquers that fear."*
— Nelson Mandela.

In the early nineties, I decided to do a parachute jump with my sister and a group of friends in aid of Ireland's largest paediatric hospital, Our Lady's Children's Hospital, Crumlin, Dublin. The mission of the hospital is to constantly improve the health and wellbeing of children and adolescents in a safe environment, which is driven by quality healthcare. I just love this idea of placing the needs of children first. When we arrived at Baldonnel Aerodrome, the group was bursting with energy and excitement. As the day progressed I listened to lectures about health and safety, where to stand as I got out of a plane 6,000 feet in the sky, what to expect when I jumped, how to check that the parachute is open, how to open the emergency parachute if the main parachute failed, and so on. The whole experience was exhilarating.

Then came the real test: getting into a small plane, going up into the sky, knowing that I was going to jump on my own, with no supports, no safety net, no way of turning back. I was afraid. The door opened, I looked out, and fear and panic quickly crept in. My breathing got faster and my mind was screaming, *"Don't do this!"* But deep down my gut told me that I was going to be okay. I had the training and skill. Now was not the time to allow fear to take over. So I jumped. Wow! What an experience, gliding through the sky at 180mph like a bird. It was my choice to jump and I had only myself to blame if anything went wrong. My sister was not as lucky as I was. She broke her leg in three places when she hit the ground. But to this day neither of us have any regrets.

When I reflect on this event and how I could apply it to my life, I think of the word 'joy'.

'J' for 'Jesus'. Did I pray during this experience? I certainly did. I prayed that all would be well and that we would reach our target to raise money for those in need.

The letter 'O' is for 'Others'. Having a spirit of generosity is a great quality to have. It is often when we reach out to others that we truly give thanks for all the good things we have in life.

'Y' for 'Yourself'. It is so important to look after your own needs before you can care for others, whether they are family, friends or people in the community.

I encourage and invite you to take time and 'Jump for Joy!'

# 19. Adventure

> *"Let us step into the night and pursue that flighty*
> *temptress, adventure."* — J.K. Rowling,
> *'Harry Potter and the Half-Blood Prince'.*

One of the first major adventures I experienced was a six-week working trip to Florida. I was there doing supply work so the local priest could have a holiday. This was really a big moment in my life. I was so excited that I packed and repacked my bags at least six times. Before heading to Shannon Airport I ensured that I had ticked all the boxes on my list. The final check was on the journey. I stopped the car to see if I had everything in order, especially passport, driver's licence, traveller's cheques (long before we had Visa cards) and of course the American dollar. Even using a different currency was going to be a new experience. This was also the time that America, along with the Allied coalition's military offensive, attacked Iraq using the name Desert Storm (1990–91). During my stay I received an invitation to join the American army as a chaplain, which involved travelling to wherever the troops were based. At one stage in my life I would have jumped at this opportunity. But now I had matured and believed a country had the right to defend itself against hostile forces but had no right to invade another country.

When I was in Florida I met some beautiful and amazing people. I walked, ran and enjoyed my time on West Palm Beach. I visited Miami city, Cape Canaveral and Tampa city. I spent time at museums, art galleries, jazz shows, Disney World and more. I felt like a computer expanding my knowledge and experience. Everything about America was different from the Ireland that we experienced in the 1980s: the roads, the cars, the shopping 'malls'. I took hundreds of photos. In those days there were no digital cameras and I had to print the photos. It didn't matter; I continued to take hundreds of photos because I wanted to show my family and friends the awesome experience I had.

When I came home, the first task was to develop my photos so I could share my experience with others and tell the stories behind the photos. That's when I hit a brick wall. I was unable to describe my experience. I had been so caught up in the taking of the photos that I lost a little piece of awe and wonder. The magic wasn't in it for me. I had travelled but did not fully engage with the experience.

I decided to try to engage more with the experience on future holidays. One such occasion was a family holiday. We decided to explore the south of France and travel down the east coast of Spain. Our first stop was to the beautiful town of Carcassonne near Perpignan which has a beautiful beach and a magnificent medieval castle. We stayed on a camping site for two weeks. We met up with another family — good friends from Ireland — who had children the same ages as us. We all had fun, laughter, late nights at karaoke singing, which was helped by a little wine tasting! On the campsite there was plenty of planned entertainment for the children.

We were sad to leave France and our friends but excitement took over as we drove towards the north of Spain; first stop was the famous Gaudi Cathedral in Barcelona. In 1882 construction began on this cathedral and it's hoped that it will be completed in 2026, the centenary of Gaudi's death. I was totally filled with a sense of awe and wonder and a deep appreciation of my faith. Of course I wanted to share this experience with my family.

After exploring the city and conquering the theme park, we headed further south and landed in the city of Valencia just in time for the Americas Cup Competition 2007. This is the oldest trophy in international sport and dates back to 1851. This was the place to find the best sailors and fastest boats in the world. This experience was so inspiring for me, it increased my interest in water sports.

Back into the car and headed down to Alicante, which was our final destination. This is a beautiful city which was inhabited for over 7,000 years. It has great history with the Greeks and Romans, and today tourists visit from all over the world. You will find a very modern city side-by-side with the old city, which is the main tourist area. As a family we fell in love with this city and have travelled back there every year since our first visit.

On this journey we visited theme parks, swam in the sea, enjoyed mud baths, refreshed ourselves in spring waters, took boat trips, went on train journeys, and visited lovely cities while exploring their museums and tasting their exotic foods. It was a fabulous trip lasting eight weeks; it cost a fortune but was worth every penny. Mind you, the driving in Spain was exhausting: firstly, I was on the opposite side of the road and secondly, on certain stretches of motorway the speed limit increased to 130 kilometres per hour. I decided that the only way to get to know a country is to explore three cities within that country — then you will have an understanding of the people, their history and culture. I found myself again taking lots of photos but I was very conscious of ensuring the children and myself were fully aware of the experience and connecting with every event.

On our return, I was sharing the photos with friends and family over dinner. My friend said, *"I can see lots of photos of the children and their mighty experience, but there are none of you."* Silently I saw this as a compliment because I had learned to engage with the experience and adventure.

## Life

Life,
Allow for vulnerability,
Allow for imperfection,
Allow for acceptance.
When I am weak,
Then I am strong.

# 20. Just A Dollar

*"The greatest legacy one can pass on to one's children and grandchildren is not money or other material things accumulated in one's life, but rather a legacy of character and faith."* — Billy Graham.

Americans love the dollar bill, which has become a symbol of their country. It stands for the American dream of Liberty, Freedom and Justice. During another trip, I was on supply work during the summer, which I really enjoyed. This time I worked in a parish in Long Island, New York. The highlight for me was celebrating daily Mass which was televised live in NY. The Archdiocese of NY had nearly three million Catholics. Part of me was so proud to be doing this work; I felt like a bit of a celebrity. But there are always moments to bring me back to reality and down to earth. One day when I was out walking taking a break, I went to the local Subway to grab a bite to eat before dashing off to work. I struck up a conversation with a local man. There had been something on the news shortly before that about the public display of religious symbols. I was wearing a little cross on my jacket and the man began speaking to me in an argumentative way, saying that he didn't believe in God and that religious symbols should not be allowed in public. He went on to say that all churches and places of worship should be closed down. Then out of his jacket pocket he produced a dollar bill. *"This is the only symbol I believe in,"* he said. I asked him to read out the inscription on the dollar bill: *"In God we trust."*

*Walking On Air* by Francis O' Toole

# 21. Lagos

*"As long as poverty, injustice and gross inequality persist in our world, none of us can truly rest."*
— Nelson Mandela.

I was fortunate to have the opportunity to visit the city of Lagos, Nigeria's largest city. Lagos is known for its beach resorts, boutiques and nightlife. You could land in this city believing that all people enjoyed great wealth. Lagos is one of the most expensive cities in the world to live in. In some parts the residents of Lagos have the highest standards of living in Nigeria and even Africa. Most of these live in very large houses. Like any city Lagos has history, culture, dance, music and sports. Unfortunately this city also has tremendous poverty. A city of two sides. I experienced and witnessed the city of poverty, hunger and injustice. There is a tremendous poverty among a large proportion of residents living in slums without access to basic piped water and sanitation. I saw many children and youths living on the streets. They were neglected by family and the state. They lived and slept at the beach, under bridges, in empty vehicles and empty buildings. Most of these lived off begging, working long hours for little money. Others procured money as a result of sexual exploitation. Those living in poverty lived a life of insecurity and even police harassment.

Charity workers and religious organisations helped where they could. This work is best witnessed in the area of education and health. Their efforts remind me of Mother Teresa of Calcutta, who once described her work as *"working with the poorest of the poor"*. A city of two worlds, wealth and poverty living side by side. But what left a profound impact on me was my experience of knowing criminal gangs were taking control of those begging on the streets. It is said that criminal organisations know as 'beggar gangs' keep children in captivity, give them little food and water while forcing them to beg. In extreme cases gangs even crippled healthy children so they would gain more sympathy from passers-by, especially tourists. Gang members could be seen in the morning dropping off children in crowded areas in the city to beg and then collecting them late in the evening, taking whatever money they had procured during the day.

I felt powerless. Even thinking about this experience generates a raw feeling within my stomach. I questioned why a loving God would not come down from the clouds and make everything right. I will never understand poverty or injustice. Yet I am aware you will find both in every city worldwide.

While in Lagos I had the opportunity to lead the local Catholic community in prayer and daily Mass. It never ceases to amaze me how people who experience real hardship and pain will cling on to their faith and not give up hope. Sunday Mass was a big occasion. People gathered in their hundreds to celebrate. On my first Sunday leaving the sacristy, the parish priest asked how long would I preach for? I told him in Ireland a sermon could last five minutes; he directed me to preach for one hour. Wow! This seemed like an impossible task. I discovered Mass and church for people on a Sunday was a really important part of their life. It allowed the people to experience normality, dress up and escape from the hard reality of poverty. For them, the celebration of Mass was all about community. The celebration of Mass could last for up to three hours and was full of song and dance. It was a humbling experience for me to witness their offertory procession as people came with items such as food, clothes, chickens, toilet rolls, etc. These people who gathered to pray also understood how to be generous and respond to the needs and cries of the poor.

My experience in Lagos had taught me to be full of gratitude for all things in life. It created within me an awareness of poverty, it created an awareness of injustice but most of all it created an awareness of survival built on the virtues of faith, hope and love.

# 22. Scholar

*"Your life is your message to the world.*
*Make it inspiring."* — Lorin L. Lee.

In 1996 I travelled to Iona College, New York. As I
embarked on a two year part-time programme studying
for my Masters of Science in Psychotherapy, I was
encouraged to write a journal and constantly reflect on the
experiences of life. I had a belief in the importance of
lifelong learning. Over the years I studied Philosophy,
Psychology, Education Management, Sociology, Theology,
Canon Law, History and Counselling. I qualified as a
teacher. My motto was: *"knowledge brings freedom"*.
From studying in so many different universities over the
years, I discovered that the most important thing for
success is to study what I choose. I cannot be or do what
other people suggest; this is not the best course of action
or even the easiest. If I embark on study, I will be the one
investing time and energy. To be enthusiastic and to ensure I
achieve my dream, I must be responsible for my decisions.
Every action and choice will have its own consequences.

During this summer in Iona College we had lectures from
9am to 9pm with short breaks in between. We remained
under pressure to stick with the programme. The pressure
was to pass all exams at the end of each course module or
repeat the modules again. Nobody wanted this, knowing
that it was expensive to study in an American college. I
strove to have a beginner's mind, attend lectures and listen
to the professors, take notes and be willing to ask
questions. The eureka moment for me came in one word:
'understanding'. In school we were taught to learn

information off by heart for exams. This involved practising the ability to recall. But when I discovered the importance of understanding the information, I never forgot what I was taught. I would recommend if you are embarking on a journey of learning, choose your path yourself, be willing to learn from your experiences and you will reach your destination.

'I am' a lover of knowledge. Learning new things has brought me to new worlds. My soul knows it will adapt to the challenges I give it. My soul needs to grow and develop. Being a scholar enables me to see the bigger picture. If I see study as a lifelong process, it will bring me to a new understanding and I discover new worlds. Knowledge is a tool to help me reach out for new horizons, to touch the sky. Reach for the stars and maybe land on the moon. As I journey in the world of academics, I set goals, I tell myself to relax and enjoy every second. The real learning is in the journey itself.

I gained so much from the interaction with other students on this course; in study groups, at sports and even when socialising, having a pint. I discovered so much about myself and how I interacted with people. I saw every experience on the course as an opportunity for self growth, discovery and learning. It was during this course that I began to question the real me, not the person who had titles or achievements. I wanted to discover me: the person with feelings, emotions, discovering strengths and acknowledging weaknesses. For the first time, I began to question my vocation to the priesthood. I realised that I ignored my humanity, I ignored my brokenness, I ignored my emotions, I ignored the right to intimacy. For the first time I felt distress that was difficult to manage; part of me felt overwhelmed. I understood that emotions were normal and that everyone experiences them but somewhere I closed off emotions. I think I did this, in a strange way, to cope with some pressures of priestly life. I was beginning a new journey, looking at myself, trying to name and identify emotions I was feeling: whether I was angry, anxious or depressed. I knew this allowed me to understand the reasons why I react the way I do in my thinking and physical reactions. I realised the importance of naming my emotion and deciding what to do first before acting on it. Instead of actions and reactions I was learning the ability to allow actions happen, reflect on the experience, then respond in whatever way I thought best.

Look at how children express themselves with faces alight when they see things for the first time. Their faces light up with excitement, passion and open eyes. I invite you to be receptive to new possibilities, not getting stuck in a rut out of your own past experience. Take on a new challenge and see everything as a new experience. Developing a pure mind, a beginner's mind, does not require you to go to college. Often our way of thinking is formed by the environment we grew up in. There is a constant danger that our beliefs about what we "know" stop us from seeing things as they really are. I am trying to cultivate a mind that is willing to see everything as if it were for the first time, to take on new challenges and to see everything as a new experience, to be open-minded. Every moment is unique; every experience is unique. I want to allow myself to be open to unique possibilities.

There will always be moments in my life when the challenge is too great or I feel like giving up because of negative outside influences. But I am prepared: I say, *"I am a scholar."* By staying with the challenge, by believing and trusting in my ability, I will reach my academic goal. I believe in having a beginner's mind, allowing myself to experience events and people I know or don't know with fresh eyes. This 'beginner's mind' concept came from Buddhism; it invites us to experience life in a new way that is unburdened by past events or previous experience. I think this means we need to be emptied of the old ways, which will allow us to be open to new ways of doing things. Look at the following: to be as a child; see everything with life, energy and passion. I believe we can enrich our lives daily if we choose to be open to seeing every experience as a learning opportunity, read books regularly and always keep a personal journal. *"Knowledge brings freedom"*.

# 23. Suicide

*"It is not the strongest of the species that survives, nor the most intelligent that survives. It is the one that is most adaptable to change."*
— Charles Darwin.

Over the years as a priest and a psychotherapist, I have spoken with many people about death, self-harm and suicide. In Ireland, we have a high rate of mental health issues and there's a very high rate of suicide amongst the young population, especially young men, who alone account for the increase in the rate of Irish suicide in the last two decades. Statistics show that suicide is highest in the USA amongst the elderly. There are possibly many reasons for this, but loneliness is the main cause. Everyone in Ireland knows of someone who died by suicide or has lost a member of their own family to suicide.

There are many people full of pain; they feel so confused and hopeless. Sadly they will pay the ultimate price by taking their own lives. Unfortunately on many occasions I was called out as a priest to anoint someone who died by suicide. I felt so powerless; a deep sadness overshadowed me. I cried out to myself in anger, *"Why could this person not call for help?"* I wonder do they feel that nobody can help them or that others would not understand their pain? It seems to me that if they can't see any other way of dealing with their difficulties, pain and hurt, suicide can seem like the only way out.

My task is to console a grieving family. I can only imagine the pain of the individual who died by suicide, which must have been so deep that they felt hopelessness, isolation and loneliness. They must have felt there was no answer to their problems. But now in a strange way, the grieving family feels the same depth of pain and hurt because they were unable to reach out to their loved one. There can be no greater grief for a parent than to see a son or daughter die by suicide. The following words by Elisabeth Kübler-Ross always give me hope when working with the bereaved:

> *"The most beautiful people we have known are those who have known defeat, known suffering, known struggle, known loss, and have found their way out of the depths. These persons have an appreciation, a sensitivity, and an understanding of life that fills them with compassion, gentleness, and a deep loving concern. Beautiful people do not just happen."*

Other people die from natural causes, accidents or illness. Whatever the cause, the loss of a loved one causes much pain. It leaves a void in our lives. It leaves us feeling stuck or full of anger. St. Augustine once said to a grieving parent, *"The child of your tears will never be wiped away."* When we love someone or have had a special relationship with them or maybe have been inspired by their work, we feel bereft when this person leaves our world, especially if it is through suicide. Yet many people will also leave this world alone with nobody to care for them or shed a tear for them.

As a society — particularly in Ireland — we need to constantly ask: why are so many young people self-harming and taking their own lives? We need to give young people belief in themselves and train them to be resilient. We have to let them know that it is okay and normal not to feel okay, and it's absolutely okay to look for help.

## Suicide

Life ended forever.
I was there,
Watching, as he hung,
Hanging like a basket from a tree.

All is lost,
With this cold shower of rain,
What a lonely spot.

Determined to climb high,
Was it impulse or carefully measured?

Maybe he did not know
Hanging can kill.
Maybe he did not know
He was going to die.

No sound of birds,
Darkness descends.
No sound of voices,
Decency remains silent.

Gardaí are called.
Notes were taken.
But none were shared.
Nobody knows what was going on in his head.

The branches now powerful.
If only they could break,
Maybe it would not be too late.
He could have life.
Why did he choose death?

In this cold spot,
I struggle to understand.
How one so young,
So full of life and love,
Drifts violently into eternity.

He will find God
Still, warm and accepting,
Embracing him into eternity,
This lost son with his life destiny.

May God be waiting
With warm peace and unconditional love,
Embrace her lost son,
With her eternal love.

# 24. Death

*"It is nothing to die. It is frightful not to live."*
— Victor Hugo, '*Les Misérables*'.

I can easily recall my Dad's final years. He was physically sick and confined to the family home. His death was a natural process and gave the family time to share special moments with him and to say their goodbyes. We all had our personal time with him, we told stories about him, looked for forgiveness if needed, said sorry for any harm done. We were lucky. His death became a celebration of life.

Even though nobody wants to talk about death, we are all aware — deep down — that one day each of us will cross that threshold. It is good to be aware that we will die. One thing I love about the Christian teaching is the belief in the afterlife. Many religions express the same belief. Our bodies return to dust but our spirit reaches into the universe. Yet deep within most of us there is a denial about the ending of life. We think very little about the shortness of our time on planet Earth. We keep ourselves busy, busy, busy, like bees hovering among the colourful plants and looking for honey. We tend to work and play as if there is no end.

As a priest, I was called on many occasions to pray over and anoint someone who had reached the final hours of their journey in this life. I have often spoken to people about their readiness or lack of readiness for death. Each one of these encounters was a sacred occasion. Some people were happy and content. They knew that they lived a good life with no regrets. Others were frightened by death, maybe because they were also frightened by life. Others regretted things they had not done, for example, being unable to extend a hand of forgiveness to a son or daughter, or being unable to say sorry for something or goodbye to someone special in their life. *"If only I had one more chance"* is something that I have often heard people say.

I always found writing about death emotional and draining. I think of all those who are no longer with us: family members, great friends, classmates, people whom I met during my ministry and people who left this world suddenly to whom I didn't get a chance to say goodbye. I will never forget the day that I was called out to anoint a good friend who was married with very young children; he lost his battle to cancer. I was heartbroken and in tears. I had no answers. I even questioned my faith but I still had to carry out my duty as a priest, to be brave and strong for others. Sudden death can come at any moment, to anyone — regardless of status or wealth.

Do not be afraid of death. Talk about death with loved ones, family and friends. If we embrace death, we will have the courage, strength and ability to live life to its fullest.

## The Morgue

I entered the morgue in silence,
The pain of grief
Cut through the air,
Easily seen in eyes full of tears.

People of all ages steered
Voiceless by the pain,
A loved one has departed.
His dream, his vision,
Gone from this earth.

Rosary beads shaking,
Trembling hands.
All wearing black,
Consumed in the grief of death.

The prayers began.
Lips mumbled,
Voices faint.
The angel of death
Could not be seen.

Blinded by tears,
A loved one gone.
Shaking hands,
Bodies, pressing close,
Giving strength.

Courage renewed.
Rising up, pain and grief.
Hope is given,
Faith and belief.

*Walking On Air* by Francis O' Toole

# 25. Good Luck, Bad Luck

*"How wonderful it is that nobody need wait a single moment before starting to improve the world."*
— Anne Frank.

There is an old Chinese story told about a poor farmer with poor land and little livestock. Every night he gathered with his neighbours around the fire to share the stories of their day. One neighbour asked the poor farmer if he was angry at the universe because his best horse had strayed and could not be found. The poor farmer replied, *"Good luck, bad luck, such is life."*

Amazingly, a few days later the stray horse returned with ten other horses. All of the neighbours gathered with excitement and asked the farmer how he felt about the universe now. *"Good luck, bad luck, such is life,"* came the reply. The farmer's oldest son worked tirelessly with the extra horses until one day one of the horses kicked him and broke his leg in two. The neighbours gathered and said to the farmer, *"Surely you believe the universe sent you bad luck with those extra horses?"* Once again the farmer gave his usual reply, *"Good luck, bad luck, such is life."* Two months later, the country went to war and all of the young men from the community were conscripted into the army. When the officers approached the poor farmer they took his horses but refused to take his son because of his broken leg. The farmer looked to the universe and said, *"Good luck, bad luck, such is life."*

What may seem to be evil on the surface could be good in disguise. Conversely, that which may seem to be good on the outside may in fact be evil. We would be wise to trust in the Creator for all of the experiences we have in life and allow him to be the judge. It would be good if we could learn to be non-judgmental, as we may never know why certain experiences or people come our way. A good businessman or a wise person sees every experience as win/win.

I served as a priest in the cathedral town of Thurles, County Tipperary for five years from 1993–98. This was a great honour for me because my family lived in the next parish, Templemore. Thurles was considered a mini-Vatican with its two seminaries, many schools, churches, clergy, Ursuline Convent, Presentation Convent and Mercy Sisters, and an Edmund Rice School. In my experience, these men and women who dedicated their life to the gospel did so with great enthusiasm, especially in the areas of education and caring for the sick. Daily Mass attendance was very high and continues to be. In the town, religion was given a special place, not forgetting of course that this is the town where Archbishop Croke and other like-minded people set up the GAA in 1884. I often refer to the faithful as 'priestly people' because we are all anointed in the Christian faith at baptism but only a few are called to serve in active ministry. We are all called to give witness to what we believe is the challenge of the gospel, *"Love your neighbour as you love yourself."* (Mark 12:31).

As an ordained priest, my duties varied, from visiting the sick, burying the dead, witnessing at marriages, baptisms and being chaplain to the local school. For me, one of the most difficult jobs was spending hours on a Saturday in a cathedral confession box listening to penitents expressing their sins. There was great trust expected here on the part of the penitent expressing their sins and for my part it was humbling to be the listener. I have no doubt about the grace of forgiveness in this sacrament when genuine penitents may experience God's grace the moment they hear the words, *"Your sins are forgiven, go in peace"*. This was an expression of God's unconditional love and forgiveness. The gift of faith is to believe. But there were times when I felt totally powerless hearing some sins knowing the person committed a crime but there was nothing I could do because I was obliged under canon law to protect the seal of confession or suffer excommunication. Often on the same day, I was called to officiate at a wedding ceremony. I always found weddings a joyful occasion. It was beautiful to witness two people in love willing to make a lifelong commitment to each other, to be there for each other in good times, in sickness and in health, in poverty or wealth. Yet their public expression of love reminded me of my inner loss of something so beautiful. It would force me to question my celibacy and remind me that I was destined to live a single life. We were told in college that celibacy was a great gift given by God. We were never told that the sacrament of marriage was even a greater gift. Of course this would often leave me feeling empty within. I had to constantly recommit myself to the promise of celibacy, which was becoming more and more a struggle. This would force me to question my comfort zone and eventually rock my cage.

At that time, as a young man with plenty of energy, the local bishop decided to give me a challenge by appointing me as Event Manager of a large community hall, the Premier Hall in Thurles. The Premier had been a famous dance hall back in the sixties and seventies. A priest colleague described my new appointment as a poisoned chalice. I was given no funds, no staff and the building was in disrepair.

With help from members of the community, I developed ways of generating finance for the hall. Along with the usual parish bingo, I got involved with Tipperary FM and hosted many famous events such as D'Unbelievables, Boyzone and singer/songwriter Kris Kristofferson. I love his song *'Help Me Make It Through The Night'*. This hall had been dead but now was being brought back to life. At one stage I had thirty people employed through a government-backed FÁS scheme. I had the opportunity to bring people together in both the church and in the community hall. Later, when the cathedral needed several months of construction work, the Premier Hall was ready to become a temporary cathedral, accommodating the priests and bishop of the parish for all liturgical services. Such were the high standards achieved that I had the hall ready, available and passed for all health and safety standards.

During this time I was appointed chaplain to the Traveller community. I was impressed by their simple but very strong faith. The Travellers had few resources: no accommodation and they often left school at a very young age, resulting in reading and writing difficulties. Unfortunately many Travellers were alienated by the settled community. A young, local Traveller couple wanted to get married. They couldn't find a venue and had been turned down by various hotels. This discrimination attracted a lot of media attention. The couple came to me for support as a chaplain and I had a solution: the Premier Hall. I approached the local hotel and discussed the matter with the owner who agreed to set up the hall as a wedding venue. Two days before the wedding, I was approached by the local Garda Superintendent. He said that the wedding couldn't go ahead since the Premier Hall had no bar/ alcohol licence.

I find it difficult to accept injustice and I believe that we must always fight for those who are vulnerable. So I decided to challenge this decision and secured a hearing in the circuit court in Limerick on the morning of the wedding. The judge requested me to stand in the witness box, an experience I'd never had before, and he asked why I was there. I clearly stated that I had been asked to come up with a solution for this young couple who could not find a venue for their wedding. I said that while they were members of an ethnic minority group, I believed that they had the right to celebrate their wedding as much as any member of the settled community. The Judge granted a licence, a precedent set in law, and a temporary alcohol licence was granted to a building with no bar licence.

By five o'clock that evening, I was back in the Premier Hall about to enjoy the starters of a beautiful meal, when an RTÉ television crew came and asked for interviews with the young couple and myself. We appeared on the RTÉ television news at 6pm, 9pm and 10:30pm. The event generated much media attention over the following months and who knows what impact it had on the following: the Employment Equality Act 1998 now stated nine grounds on which discrimination is outlawed: gender, marital status, family status, sexual orientation, religion, age, race, disability and membership of the travelling community. In 2000 the Law on Equality was set up in Ireland.

Good luck, bad luck, such is life.

## Dreams

In my dreams you are there,
When I awake you are here,
Each time I think of you
I love you
More.

# 26. Crossroads

**"The meaning of life is to find your gift.
The purpose of life is to give it away."**
— Pablo Picasso.

Leaving the priesthood was a bigger decision than joining the seminary sixteen years before. When I joined the seminary, I was innocent, I was full of idealism and had a simple faith. There was excitement and hope and trepidation about the unknown. I was very fortunate to have had ten years in active ministry, during which I had gained experience, wisdom and lots of joy. Deciding to leave was a major decision and brought a deep sadness and real pain into my life.

When I first started to question my calling to active ministry. I was unhappy with the way the official church was not dealing with scandals within the church.

Some priests inflicted terrible damage on young children. We now know that many bishops and others in authority have been accused of covering up cases of sexual abuse. They were willing to cover up scandals and move priests to a different parish when there was an accusation in order to avoid negative publicity. What a shame that we protected those who committed such evil acts of betrayal. It is now clear that many bishops only wanted to protect the good name of the church. They forgot about the message of the gospel which clearly speaks about justice, leading a good life, and caring for the poor and vulnerable. No bishop was civilly prosecuted for covering up for a priest accused of sex abuse in Ireland. Worldwide no bishop was forced to resign his position.

Most of the men and religious I worked with were good people, full of compassion. They had great vision. I, like many others, found it difficult to be on the front line daily working within parishes, facing parishioners every morning. I tried to put on a brave face despite feeling disgust at the latest scandal that had hit the church. I constantly found myself defending the indefensible. I, like many others, hoped that whatever scandal was revealed today would be gone tomorrow. But scandals continued like a tidal wave, hitting the Irish church and churches worldwide. I found myself constantly apologising to people for the offences of others. Parishioners rightly and justifiably wanted answers.

For the first time I felt alone, unable to cope with social pressure. I also began to question my promise of celibacy. The church called celibacy a gift of faith which would help us to follow in the footsteps of Christ. I began to question whether this was really true or whether the church was protecting its material wealth. St. Peter, the first Pope, and the apostles that Jesus chose were for the most part married men. It was over 300 years later that the church first began to think about the life of a priest and whether they could be married or not. Priests — even Popes — still continued to get married and have children right up until the second Lateran council in 1139. After that date, celibacy was mandated under canon law for the universal church.

The Eastern Catholic church, which is recognised by the Vatican, still has married priests and in England Anglican married clergy can join the Catholic church as ordained priests, thanks to the insight of St. John Paul II. A friend who worked in the Westminster diocese in London dedicated twelve years to priestly work, but he had to leave the priesthood to get married only to be replaced by a married Anglican priest. So why not allow all priests have the option to remain celibate or get married? With such heavy issues to confront daily, I became increasingly frustrated, annoyed and confused in my ministry. I went to bed at night exhausted and woke up convincing myself, *"Today is a new day, give it everything."*

Then somewhere I realised that it could not be right to be constantly pushing myself. I wanted to be authentic, real and accountable for all my actions. I decided to take action. I needed time out to reflect on everything that was going on in my heart and mind. I was at the crossroads of my life and unsure of my direction. I arranged to have an appointment with the bishop in May 1998. He agreed to see me in the bishop's palace built by Bishop Butler circa 1785; it is a beautiful and commodious building attached to the cathedral in Thurles. What luxury! It's baffling to think one man could live in such a place on his own and be content. The walls featured priceless paintings; the house was full of antiques. The housekeeper arranged a cup of tea served in lovely delph. Well, the bishop got straight to the point by asking, *"What did I want?"* I felt so nervous, my mind was racing and my heart beating so fast. I proceeded to express my thoughts, my concerns, I talked about celibacy and how I was confused; I said my confusion was not helped by that fact that I had been sexually abused in the seminary. I said that right now I was exhausted and needed some time out to reflect on my future. He listened very carefully to everything I said — then out of the blue he had an answer. Would I be willing to go to the USA and work in a parish there? I thought this was really funny: ten years previously I would have jumped with excitement at such an offer. But now it felt like a consolation prize. My mind was racing. I came to the conclusion that the bishop was giving me the message, *"You failed, now go and sort yourself out."* This, of course, was my perception of the experience. I know my pain and hurt was not heard.

Deep down I was tired of running. Now I just wanted to face all the issues in my life and tackle each, one by one. I declined the offer and suggested that with his support I would go to Dublin and get a part-time job. This was not good enough; his next sentence surprised me, *"If you get a job, you will not need the diocese to support you."* There in that moment, after serving the church for sixteen years, I was deflated. I left with little or no satisfaction, no suggestions, no plan of action. I headed back to the presbytery and informed my colleagues to their surprise, that I was taking time out. I then visited my parents to inform them of my decision…were they disappointed!

What a day! I drove towards Dublin. Back then the roads were very poor and the journey from Thurles to Dublin took over three hours but felt like thirty hours. This was a long drive; my mind kept replaying the actions of the day. I arrived at the outskirts of Dublin and stopped at the Green Isle Hotel to gather myself. I must have been an emotional wreck. I had no plan, no accommodation. I took deep breaths to calm myself. I took out a pen and paper to try to work out an action plan.

Then I had a eureka moment, I went straight to the manager of the hotel and asked if they needed a barman. This is what I would call 'a walk-in interview'. I got the job. The day had been a roller coaster, beginning with celebrating Mass in Thurles Cathedral and ending serving pints to customers in a Dublin hotel.

Thankfully, at the end of the summer, I got a job teaching religion and counselling in Belvedere College, Dublin. It was here that I met my wife-to-be. Falling in love is a magical moment. For me it was the answer to all my problems. Suddenly I was not alone and for the first time felt the presence of another's intimacy to empower me.

For me intimacy was about meeting another person's soul to share, care, have a common story. I wanted our souls to meet and walk the journey of life together as a couple. There were times when I had an irrational shame and guilt for leaving the priesthood. I felt I had let my colleagues down. It took me a while to understand that intimacy is the greatest gift and can offer the greatest challenge in life.

That same year, I applied to the National University of Ireland, Maynooth, and to Trinity College to study for the Higher Diploma in Education which would allow me to teach in a secondary school and be employed by the Department of Education. During this time I also applied to be laicized by the church from my priesthood: this involved interviews, psychological tests and finally to swear an oath not to discuss any details in public. Once again the church sought secrecy.

I had left the security of the church which controlled my thinking and feeling for sixteen years. Or maybe I should say I allowed the church to be in control. Now I was free to make my own choices and take on new responsibilities. I was offered a place to study the H. Dip in Education at the National University of Ireland, Maynooth (NUIM) and at Trinity College, Dublin. I was familiar with Maynooth. At that time I knew very little about Trinity, only that from 1871 to 1970 the Catholic church in Ireland forbade its members to attend Trinity. I was fearful in case I would make a wrong decision. Still I faced my fear and did it anyway. I decided on Trinity College. I will always remember the day I walked through those famous gates: it felt like a dark tunnel. Then out of darkness came the light, a new beginning of academic learning. Deep down it all felt good.

When I told my mother I was going to Trinity, she couldn't believe it. She was a woman of her time and was convinced that I was going totally against my religion to join the Protestant church. Thankfully, Ireland has moved on.

That was a great academic year and during the Christmas season my daughter Zoe was born. This was the greatest gift I ever received. I felt so alive, a new man. I can recall getting up at night to feed her, looking at college notes at 3am (this was probably the only quiet time I was going to get for myself), then getting up later at 6:30am to get ready before heading into college. There were times when I was really tired fulfilling the daily routines but I never got tired of the work or responsibilities. I found that year exciting, challenging and life-giving.

To become a parent was the greatest feeling of joy and achievement in my life. My title had changed from 'Father' to 'Daddy'.

## Love

> Heart that shares,
> Eyes that smile,
> Ears that listen,
> Voice that supports,
> Smell that beauty,
> Drinks from shared cup.

# 27. Belief

*"You never know when one kind act or word of encouragement can change a life forever."*
— Zig Ziglar.

There is a story told about a farmer who loved a bit of excitement in his farming day. One day when out walking on his farm, the farmer decided to climb a cliff above the valley to see what lay beyond. He climbed for hours until he reached a ledge just below the top of the cliff. There, to his amazement, was a nest full of eagle's eggs. He was delighted and, even though he knew it was unfair to the birds and illegal, he carefully took a single egg, stowed it in his backpack, climbed back down the cliff and returned to his farm.

When he got home, he put the egg in with the few chickens he kept in the yard. The mother hen was the proudest bird you ever saw, sitting atop this magnificent egg, and the cockerel couldn't have been prouder. A few weeks later, the egg hatched and out came a little bird. Because the chickens were happy with this new bird, they said nothing and brought the bird up as one of their own.

The eagle grew up with its brother and sister chicks. It learned to do all the things chickens do: clucking and cackling, scratching in the dirt for grit and worms, flapping its wings furiously and flying just a few feet in the air before crashing down to earth in a pile of dust and feathers. Of course, the little eagle believed it was a chicken. He would see amazing beautiful birds flying in the air above with grace and magnificence. The little bird would sigh and say, *"I am only a chicken and we chickens are birds of the earth and not of the sky. "* He would then cast his eyes down and continue to dig in the dirt.

Whenever I told the story of the eagle, people expected a different ending, with the eagle soaring and flying according to his true potential. So often, unfortunately, we believe what we hear and learn about our limitations. The right kind of encouragement will help us to flourish, especially if we have doubts about ourselves or if we're not coping with the challenges life presents us with. If we don't receive encouragement there is always the danger that negative thinking and negative feelings will prevent us from achieving our short-term goals and long-term dreams. I was very lucky to receive encouragement from people during school, from my family, in college and in my working life. It's incredible to think that a gentle smile of support or the right words at the right time can mean so much. My life is full of moments when I was about to give up on a project, but a kind word of encouragement changed my negative thinking into something positive and powerful. Words of encouragement may be as simple as *"don't give up"* or *"believe you can do it"*. It may come from a loved one who gives their unconditional support expressed in a hug or smile.

I've had many times when positive words of encouragement prevented me from giving up. When I was completing my postgraduate studies in Guidance Counselling at the Marino Institute of Education, part of me felt totally overwhelmed with all the changes in my life. I was ready to give up the course. The director Br. Leo took me to one side to give advice. I told him I felt stressed, full of anxiety and panicking about exams so I just wanted to drop out. With a gentle smile on his face he told me I was doing great and would get through the exams with no problems. He told me to imagine I was in a tunnel: you can't stop — you must keep going to get out. Now I know that there are times we cannot see the light at the end but it is there and the only way to see it is to go through the tunnel. Every step and positive action I took brought me closer to the end of the tunnel. I keep this image in mind whenever I get distressed. I try not to act the old way in panic but try to see things in a new way and accept that the negative experience, whatever it is, will pass.

I may have had a long career with many changes. I may have experienced brokenness in relationships and during sickness, but the support and kind words of family, friends and work colleagues have always encouraged me to keep going. My career was blessed with many opportunities, events and experiences. The guidance of others has encouraged me to stretch my boundaries and try new things rather than listening to the limitations that others have put on themselves. Let us be generous with compliments: it will help others grow and flourish; mol an óige agus tiocfaidh sí.

# 28. Travelling

*"The greatest danger for most of us is not that our aim is too high and we miss it, but that it is too low and we reach it."* — Michelangelo.

I love travelling. When I'm in a different country I always visit a centre of culture, history and music. I had a wonderful experience travelling through part of the Sahara Desert on a camel's back while in Tunisia. In Nigeria I watched an artist paint, using mud in bright colours to develop a masterpiece.

There are certain things I will not find in books or on the internet. I must explore them for myself. Having the gift of awe and wonder will create a sparkle in my eye. It will lift my heart and open my mind to new ways of doing things. 'I am' a traveller, always fascinated by different cultures, values and belief systems. The next time you travel, I invite you to write about your experience, what you encounter, the people you journey with and any insights gained. Then when you sit at a table with your family or friends, you can share what you gained and enlighten others with the stories of your travels and create a rich experience for all gathered.

During meditation I often visualise myself in another part of the world. It could be in a place I am familiar with or in another part of the world that I have never travelled to but hope to someday. The meditation allows my soul to journey into other lands, crossing skies and walls; no barriers can hold it back.

Meditation has no set goals but allows me to be fully me, accepting me as 'I am'. Meditation also allows me to be non-striving, accepting the moment for what it is and this brings real peace and happiness. I have found through daily meditation and visualisation, by placing myself in the moment, sitting back in silence or listening to quiet music, this gives great strength of mind and, dare I say, it has allowed my soul to change the universe to meet my needs.

# 29. Teaching

**"*Everybody who is incapable of learning has taken to
teaching.*"** — Oscar Wilde.

Over three hundred years ago the Burmese army planned
an invasion of Thailand. At that time the country was
known as Siam. The Siamese Monks were in possession
of a giant statue of Buddha. This statue was over ten feet
tall, weighed nearly two tonnes and was made of gold.
The monks wanted to protect the statue so they covered it
in twelve inches of mud so that no army personnel would
have an interest in it. Sadly, the monks were slaughtered in
the invasion but the army had no interest in a statue
covered in clay. The real secret of the statue died with the
monks.

In the 1950s the monastery was relocated to make room
for a highway. The monks arranged for a crane to come
and move the clay Buddha to its new location. The clay
statue was so heavy that the monks left the statue in a safe
place and covered it with sheets to protect it from rain and
moisture. That night, a monk shone his light on the statue
and noticed something shining. He called the other monks.
They immediately tried to clear away the clay and hours
later they discovered with great joy that the statue was
made of pure gold. The statue resides today in the Temple
of the Golden Buddha in Bangkok, Thailand and it is
visited every year by millions of people.

I was very touched when I heard this story. It reminds me
of the hidden beauty of all people. Sometimes we have to
dig deep to find the beauty within. We all need to spend

time shaking off the dust to find our inner strength and gold. Working as a teacher at secondary level can be challenging but rewarding. School is a place where young people find structure, safety and security. In the right environment they will flourish. This is the function of the teacher: to empower the student to discover their own gifts and talents. There is no doubt that school places a lot of pressure on teenagers in preparing for exams. Yet it never ceases to amaze me how young people can learn through the gift of fun. Fun allows for creativity and encourages us to take positive risks. Through fun and play, we create wonder, we ask questions and we don't hold back. We learn to find different and new ways of doing things. There is nothing greater than watching or listening to a young person full of laughter and fun. This fun aspect in education allows us to take down the barriers and masks that we all build up during the course of our lives. For me, play and fun touch off the Divine Spirit within. It is this Spirit that creates a flow of energy and reveals our hidden gifts. You can easily witness this in a music class, for example, where music and song touch off our emotions of love, sadness and even anger. These same songs and music which touch our souls allow us to connect with the Divine. They inspire us to celebrate and to give praise. You can find the soul full of fun in the art class where students use colour, textures, scent, feelings and purpose to give expression to their inner selves, inside out.

In every class within the school environment students will challenge themselves to find expression and discover who they are on their journey of life. I recall one day during a religion class having a great debate on world religions. At the end of the discussion a student said that she was glad to be a Christian and not a Jew. I responded, *"The first Christian, Christ, was a Jew."* In searching for truth, developing our talents and looking deep into our souls, always allow time for a bit of fun. I invite you to always value yourself and others, dig deep, you will find gold in every person you meet.

# 30. Bread

*"In the Eucharist a communion takes place that corresponds to the union of man and woman in marriage. Just as they become 'one flesh' so in Communion we all become 'one spirit', one person, with Christ."* — Pope Benedict XVI.

Navan town is twinned with an Italian town, Broccostella. Recently I visited this town along with a group of students from Loreto after winning the 2017 bursary competition Ezio Lupo award. Ezio was a 20-year-old student who died in a road traffic accident in Navan in 2004. When we arrived in Broccostella we were greeted warmly by the Lord Mayor Sergio Cippitelli, members of the council, teachers and parents from the community. During that week we had many educational experiences; to mention one, our visit to Montecassino Abbey. It is here that St. Benedict established his first monastery around 529. The hilltop abbey was the site of the battle of Monte Cassino in 1944, when the building was destroyed by Allied bombing and rebuilt after the war. It's hard to believe that anyone wanted to bring destruction to something so beautiful. This was a place where monks believed in *ora & labora* (work & prayer). It reminded me, that out of any great tragedy comes great opportunity; we should never give up; that goodness can override the badness.

I often wondered why Jesus used bread and wine as the elements at the Last Supper. I reflected on this while thinking about the motto *ora & labora*. Bread is made from grains of wheat and wine is made from grapes. From Italy to Ireland and around the world, many use bread daily as food. We also know that many use wine to celebrate success or to help heal pain. It's amazing to think both bread and wine have a journey of suffering before they reach the family table.

Wheat has to survive through the rigours of winter, then it is ground in a mill, then it is placed in hot ovens for baking. While enjoying the heat of Italy, I now understand that seeds of grapes have to burst with life through the earth in very hot climates, survive and then be crushed to create wine. We use wine to celebrate and we also use wine to commiserate. The story of Calvary is about life being crushed but something amazing followed. The resurrection, Christ transformed.

Maybe the next time you are at table, breaking bread and sharing wine, you might celebrate your life and know that you are part of God's great plan. Jesus, who experienced pain on Calvary, giver of life, wants to empathise with your pain and celebrate your success. This same Creator wants you to discover your strengths within and find tools on the outside to enable you on your journey of transformation.

# 31. Relationships

*"Nobody can hurt me without my permission."*
— Mahatma Gandhi.

When your soul touches the soul of another human being, this is a special moment. There are millions of people on the planet but love brings us into a deep and special relationship with the one person we want to share our daily lives with. At the birth of each of my children, I immediately fell in love with them. There are different types of love, best explained by the Greek philosophers.

> Eros: Love of the body. Eros was the Greek God of love and sexual desire.

> Philia: Love of the mind, also known as brotherly love. Philia represents sincere and platonic love.

> Ludus: Playful love.

> Pragma: Longstanding love.

> Agape: Love of the soul.

> Philautia: Love of the self.

> Storge: Love of the child.

I have been so lucky during the journey of my life to have met people I loved and people who have loved me. I have friends who are supportive of me and I can never repay their kindness and generosity.

I have experienced beautiful, meaningful love relationships. I have experienced falling in love with a woman who touched my soul and inspired me. I have also loved some women with all my heart and mind and experienced rejection, pain and discomfort. I have loved men — not in a sexual way — but I've loved them for their great inspiration, their vision and their philosophy of life.

In love we are touched by the Divine; something greater than ourselves brings us beyond the impossible. In love the best is brought out of us in care, nurturing and sharing dreams.

## Woman

Her presence
Creates a
Warm glow,
Like the morning sun
Glides on the horizon,

Bringing light
To a darkened world.
The sound of her voice echoes
The symphony orchestra,
Bringing joy to the world.

Her shining eyes, reflecting
Astounding beauty.
Each time I think of her
I fall in love
More.

Her gentle movement,
Her actions bringing vibrations,
Creating ripples, changing the tides
Of the mighty
Universe.

Her epic expression,
Attitudes and gratitudes
Bringing the best from others
To believe in themselves,
The power of something greater.

Her skin
White like snow
Captures pure and gold.
Her spirit, resembles the beauty of a butterfly
Dancing in the breeze

As she interacts with friends,
Family,
Foe alike.
She brings
Harmony, peace and tranquillity.

Individual and connected
Like the Grace of Trinity,
She personifies
Divinity.

*Walking On Air* by Francis O' Toole

# 32. Miracles

*"There are only two ways to live your life. One is as though nothing is a miracle. The other is as though everything is a miracle."* — Albert Einstein.

When asked by adults and students, *"Do miracles really happen?"* I first try to explain my understanding of a miracle. It is when something extraordinary happens. It goes against the laws of nature. Science cannot explain what took place. As Christians, we say that God has intervened. Maybe the real question is, *"Should we believe in miracles?"* This is more difficult to answer.

I believe we experience miracles constantly and daily but, most of the time, we fail to see them. I can easily recall the excitement and sense of peace I experienced on the birth of my children. Every time I see a flower budding and coming into full bloom I am reminded of the miracle of life.

Each day nature offers so many new things in its creation but do we really see them? I asked a group of people with whom I was working in mindfulness, *"How many petals are there on a daffodil?"* It took a while before they came up with the right answer. We may see and hear things but not be truly aware of them or observe their beauty. I once saw an experiment which illustrates this point beautifully. The famous violinist Joshua Bell 'busked' in a subway station in Washington DC. Thousands of people passed by without so much as a look at him. They were so caught up with their lives that they didn't recognise him or appreciate his artistic value. In the second part of the experiment,

Bell performed again in the same subway station. The event was widely advertised and thousands of paying customers gathered to listen to the famous violin player. Because we are all so busy, we can easily miss the daily miracles of life as we pass by.

When my daughter Zoe was born, she was very sick and diagnosed with severe chronic congenital neutropenia. She was not producing white blood cells and was constantly open to infection. As a result, she spent half of her baby life in hospital receiving treatment. She was being treated with a drug called G-CSF, which was given to patients receiving chemotherapy, as it stimulated the white blood cells from the bone marrow. Being the Dad, I had to become very brave and inject my daughter daily with this drug, a task I was never comfortable with. I prayed daily for answers and a miracle.

This was a difficult time for the whole family. I found it so stressful and frightening. I never knew what was coming next. It was so difficult to be brave trying to put on a happy smile when in fact I was falling apart on the inside. Both physically and mentally I was tired. I was exhausted from not getting enough sleep. I was weary from changing bedclothes and using the washing machine every time my daughter got sick. One night I changed the bedclothes three times. There were nights when I had to sleep sitting up with my baby on my chest so she would be comfortable and relaxed. I was weary of rushing to the hospital when my daughter had a high temperature. I was worn out watching nurses constantly checking and re-checking her bloods. I was tired of sleeping at night-time on a hospital chair. In fact, she spent three Christmases in hospital.

On the third Christmas I told her I would stay up all night Christmas Eve and watch out for Santa. Early in the morning I headed down to the small kitchen provided by the hospital for parents, needing to grab a cup of coffee before she would wake up. On my return she was jumping in the bed with excitement, Santa had called and given her a big cuddly reindeer. The tears of joy flooded my eyes. Every year this reindeer is brought out with all the Christmas decorations. It was not easy to keep my faith at this time but it was my only hope. I was angry with God; I wrestled in my thoughts about his existence. I certainly waived in my belief that God has a plan for us all. Why would he abandon me when we needed him so much? In the end, all I could do was make an act of faith, to believe he was with us in our pain.

Then, after three years of suffering, our prayers seemed to be answered. We were presented with the idea of saving stems cells from the placenta at the birth of her younger brother. The cells would be transfused into my daughter and it was hoped this would help her situation. When my son Micah was born, stem cells were saved from the placenta for this purpose. It was the first time that this had been done in Ireland.

I stopped administering the G-CSF to my daughter one week before the procedure was to take place. Two days before the operation she had a routine blood check and it appeared that her bloods had altered in a positive way and she was now producing her own white blood cells. The radical procedure never took place and the stem cells are still on ice fourteen years later. My faith and belief in miracles was finally restored.

I invite you to take a moment to stop and become totally aware of the present moment and discover the gifts and miracles all around you.

Stop; take one minute to reflect.

Take a deep breath; breath is the anchor of the body.

Observe your thoughts — what are you thinking: is it about the past or the future? Just embrace your thoughts in a non-judgmental way.

Proceed with caution — we need to start breaking old habits and create new habits.

Really connect with the world around you and then see what answer you would give to the question: *"Do miracles really happen?"*

# 33. Wake Up and Smell the Coffee

*"Life is either a daring adventure or nothing at all."*
— Helen Keller.

I'm sitting in a hospital canteen writing this piece and nursing a cup of coffee. Hospital staff come and go. They grab their coffees and scones before rushing off to their next duty. The hospital environment is a busy place. Patients are admitted under huge pressure. Sickness has taken them from their normal routine and placed them into a caring environment, where nobody really wants to be. Over the years I have visited many people, young and old, in hospital. Some had been in short term while others were less fortunate with hospital stays and appointments becoming a part of their daily routine.

For many of us sickness will come our way as a result of outside influences. For others sickness will come because of a lifetime of neglecting physical and spiritual needs. The physical building of a hospital is a reminder to all of us that we are fragile. Human beings have great courage and strength, but when sick — whether with a major or minor problem — we become vulnerable; our pride and dignity can easily be taken away. When we live a life that is not in touch with our basic needs, disengaged from the world around us, or if we live a life always reacting to an event we will be drained, burned out and in time end up mentally or physically sick.

It is my belief that most of us — in fact 80% of us — sleepwalk through life. How many times have you heard people saying, *"I did that in my sleep"*? It could be driving a car or carrying out a routine activity at work. It is the same when applied to most principles in life. We get up in the morning, wash, dress, have breakfast and head off on our daily routine, whether college, work, study, school. In the evening time we arrive home tired, we comfort eat, watch TV and head to bed exhausted. The next day the same dance is repeated. Now there is absolutely nothing wrong with this; human beings need routine, we are creatures of habit.

For me the unquestioned life or the life that has not faced major challenges is the life of a person just going through the motions. However, on the other hand, you will find that 20% of people are highly motivated, radical thinkers and shakers. This 20% are not happy with the normal routine; in fact, when they become aware that they are forming a habit, they go out of their way to break the old habit and create new ones. These people are fully alive, engaged and connected with the world around them. They develop active minds, have good health, probably have many hobbies and make lots of money. The great thing about this theory is that we all have choices. We can all decide today to choose to live life as part of that 20% who live extraordinary lives or we can remain with the other 80% who are just surviving.

How many of us drink coffee just for the sake of it? We often drink coffee to become motivated or energised. I think that dashing back a cup of coffee sends the wrong message to our brain. We are telling our brains that we need this drug to function better. The brain becomes dependent on this cup of coffee, which is doing little to help our physical bodies or our mental health. In this case I use the cup of coffee only as a metaphor to explain how we may or may not be fully alive. For some it may be coffee, for others prescribed drugs or alcohol.

How do you nurse your cup of coffee? Can you smell it before drinking it? The next time you hold a cup of coffee in your hand, feel the warmth, smell, taste, etc. By doing this, you will allow your senses to become fully alive.

My sense of touch is awakened.

My sense of taste is awakened.

My sense of sight is awakened.

My sense of smell is awakened.

My sense of hearing is awakened.

Creating this type of awareness will bring you into the 20% group of people who are fully alive, active and engaged with life. When events take place, you will not react but become more reflective and then respond to the event. Waking up and smelling the coffee means to be fully awake, to be a radical thinker, a radical mover. By creating such awareness, life becomes more exciting and less sickening. You will change your body's state, speak with authority, stand tall, and be powerful and confident. When I exude confidence people respond to me in the same way, looking at someone fully alive and engaged.

Try monitoring yourself on the following:

- Timing — knowing when to speak and knowing when not to.
- Listening — dropping what is going on in your mind and really hearing what the other person is saying.
- Agenda — stop having an agenda and work where others are at.
- Confidence — place your attention on maximising the other person's position. Give them what they need: you take the seat of power.

Meditation and daily exercise are keys to life success. Wake up, smell the coffee, choose not to allow sickness become part of your life, develop total awareness and allow yourself to become the amazing person that you truly are.

### Little Boy

Tap, Tap, Tap.
Like the beating of a
Drum,
The little boy's
Feet
Find balance as he
Runs.

# 34. Seedlings

*"Each time a man stands up for an ideal, or acts to improve the lot of others, or strikes out against injustice, he sends forth a tiny ripple of hope; and crossing each other from a million different centres of energy and daring, those ripples build a current that can sweep down the mightiest walls of oppression and resistance."*
— Robert Kennedy.

As a guidance counsellor working in a school environment, you have to be prepared for the unexpected. However, nothing can prepare you when tragedy hits your school, resulting in the loss of life. Our school experienced a black day in our history when a school bus crashed in Navan, County Meath in May 2005. The buses were doing the ordinary school runs, bringing the students home from school to their local communities. One of the buses carrying fifty-one young people was involved in a collision shortly after leaving the school. The bus came upon roadworks, went out of control, skidded and over-turned on the Navan to Kentstown Road, causing the devastating death of five young girls aged between 15 and 18. Four of the girls were from our school, Loreto, Navan.

Anyone who has experienced the death of a loved one, especially when it is so sudden, can tell of the grief and shock. Although many of the students involved in the Kentstown bus accident were lucky to escape with their lives, they were traumatised by the events they witnessed that day. These students experienced feelings associated with post-traumatic stress. Some felt guilt and shame because they were alive and their friends were dead. Some had an inability to recall things as well as they had previously and had poor concentration. They experienced a deep fear of breaking down or losing control. They blamed themselves, saying they *"should have saved more"* or *"should have acted differently"*. Some avoided the scene of the accident. Others had nightmares or were unable to eat.

The following September I wanted to create something that would be of benefit to the students who had survived the bus tragedy and would help them recover from the horror of that day. Thankfully, at that time the Principal was brave enough to go with the idea of a therapy group within the school and went out of her way to support the students. I can only salute her for the leadership and wisdom she displayed. I met with the students in Loreto, Navan and invited them to come to this weekly therapeutic group. Our first decision was to give the group a name and we called it 'Seedlings', meaning new life and new beginnings. The group included fourteen students from St. Michael's who had survived the bus accident. In facing their grief the students became survivors. They became aware of their deep pain and the pain of others who had survived the tragedy. There was no set programme to follow in dealing with such terrible pain. The group was willing to trust in the process and to trust me as their leader. This was a very humbling experience for me.

After meeting weekly for seven months the 'Seedlings' wanted an action plan put in place. As a group we embarked on a journey of promoting road safety campaigns and raising money for the hospitals of Drogheda and Navan. This was the students' way of saying thank you to everyone who had engaged with them and helped them on to new beginnings. The 'Seedlings' wanted to be positive even though they had experienced one of the worst tragedies possible. They came up with the idea of developing key rings, each bearing the motto 'life is a gift — drive with care'. The key rings had five stars to represent each of the five girls who had lost their lives. The key ring also stressed five different aspects of road safety: Awareness, Caution, Distance, Life and Safety. The first letter of each word represented the names of the girls who died on that day. The seedling group wanted to sell the key rings locally with the help of the student body. The community gave generously and rushed to buy them.

On the day of the official launch of the key ring in May 2006 the media interest was far beyond our expectations. RTÉ, TV3, Sky Ireland and the local and national papers all covered the event. Noel Brett of the Road Safety Authority and Bishop Michael Smith launched the key ring. The Seedlings group was soon inundated with requests from schools around the country and from third level institutions. Incredibly, within just one week the key rings had sold out. Because of this campaign 'Seedlings' increased road safety awareness and raised over €18,000. The money was donated to Drogheda and Navan hospitals, and a proportion allotted to covering the cost of a portable ventilator and cardiac monitor for children. Money continued to flow into the school and went into the provision of pastoral care and the purchase of two defibrillators.

Despite the pain, grief and unbelievable loss of the victims' families, friends, communities and the school, the Seedling group grew from despair and provided the five girls who died in the crash with an amazing legacy. The machines bought for the two hospitals have saved countless lives over the last eleven years. The Seedling group brought many people together within the school community and gave some hope to the families and the communities from which the five girls came.

The Seedling group reminds us that faith, hope and charity are cardinal virtues that bring goodness and communities together. These girls showed bravery, resilience and gave hope to many. It is no surprise that the Seedling group went on to win the Young People of the Year Award and the National Rehab Person of the Year Award.

*"And flights of angels sing thee to thy rest!"*
— Shakespeare's '*Hamlet*', Act 5, Scene 2.

# 35. Sitting in the Presence of Two Millionaires

**"Wealth is the ability to fully experience life."**
— Henry David Thoreau.

Not long ago I was at a lunch to honour people within our community for their great achievements and contributions locally and nationally. I happened to be seated between two men who I knew were very wealthy and worth more than fifty million euro between them. At first I was a little nervous in this company. At the time I was on the critical illness/sick leave list and my wages had been cut. As I thought about these men's wealth and my lack of it, my behaviour changed. My self-esteem dipped, my energy was low and I didn't want to engage with them.

I realised that I was creating conflict within myself. I was denying my real feelings and allowing my mind's perception of things to change my behaviour, attitudes and feelings. I had gone from being enthusiastic about the occasion to being critical and negative.

Then I pinched myself on the leg and said to myself, *"I am equal to everyone at this table."* In that moment of consciously choosing to change my thinking, my behaviour and emotions also changed. I became more positive, energetic and creative. I became the 'real me', full of honesty, sincerity and truth. I stopped my mind creating stories that were affecting me negatively. I accepted that here was a group of people enjoying sitting at a table, sharing food, telling stories, listening to the announcements of awards and hearing the experiences of the recipients.

When I relaxed and accepted my vulnerability, I became engaged. We are all vulnerable from time to time, especially when in the presence of people who may have had different life experiences or backgrounds to us. If we can become aware of our vulnerability, we can be more accepting of ourselves and others quickly and without judgement. When we can embrace ourselves as we are, we are open to loving ourselves in a non-judgemental way and to seeing the beautiful gift that we are.

# 36. The Just Man

**"Truth never damages a cause that is just."**
— Mahatma Gandhi.

There is a story told about a very wealthy businessman who wanted to build the best house in the land. He summoned all the local builders to hear their ideas and proposals before making his decision regarding the contract. After what seemed like a long time he made his choice of builder and gave him total responsibility for building this mansion. The wealthy man requested that the builder use the best of materials — regardless of the cost — and not contact him until the mansion was completed.

The builder got to work immediately but greed, envy and bitterness were deep-rooted in his belly. In order to increase his profit, he used cheap materials and knowingly bought bricks of inferior quality. The overall workmanship was extremely poor. He took shortcuts where possible, even with the roof and windows, all to make more money for himself. The more the builder was able to get away with, the more neglectful he became. Deep in his heart the builder knew that the house would not last and would produce many problems as time went on.

On the day of completion the wealthy businessman came with great excitement to greet the builder. *"My friend,"* he said to the builder, *"I trusted you with a very valuable gift: to create the house of my dreams."* To the surprise of everyone the businessman announced that since the builder had dedicated one whole year of his life to building what appeared to be a beautiful home, he wanted to give the builder the house as a gift. Can you imagine the effect this had on the builder? If only he had built the best house possible, he would be happy forever. Now he knows this house will cause him many problems and a lot of pain.

The just man will always be happy. When we do right by other people, obey the laws of the land, show kindness and love, and express forgiveness, we are being authentic and reaching our full potential.

When reflecting on my life I ask is it a house where the foundations are built on values of justice, honesty and hard work? Whatever happens, let's not build walls that divide, separate and alienate.

# 37. Optimistic

**"We are all in the gutter, but some of us are looking at the stars."** — Oscar Wilde.

There is a story told about an optimist and a pessimist. They were both in a tight security prison with limited time to socialise and exercise. One day the pessimist looked out the window of his cell and said, *"All I see is mud on the ground and chains tied to prisoners' feet."* However, the optimist looked out the same window and said, *"I can see the beautiful colour of the rainbow, the magic of the flowing clouds and birds fluttering in the breeze."*

The last four years have been difficult for me. I went through a marriage breakup, which was traumatic for all involved, both the adults and children. I succeeded in getting a church annulment, which granted great personal freedom. The annulment brought closure to a broken marriage and allowed myself and my ex-wife to move on with our lives. The whole experience had a devastating effect on my well-being, my mental health and left me in dire financial difficulty. I lost two beautiful homes, one on the east coast of Ireland and the other on the east coast of Spain. Thankfully, I had tremendous support from friends, family and three beautiful, amazing teenagers.

My daughter Zoe would often ask me what career path she should follow. I would respond by saying, *"God has big plans for you."* With a smile on her face she would ask, *"What is that plan?"* and I'd tell her that she had to discover it for herself. My sons Leon and Micah are big Lego and music fans, and it always fascinates me how they could spend hours on their own in a world of Lego and music being creative and full of imagination. Every time I think of the three teenagers, I fall in love with them more and more.

'I am' vulnerable. There is always the urge when a relationship breaks down to run as far as possible. Sometimes the pain is so great I may be justified in doing this. On the other hand, it is very rewarding to stand with my children, face my responsibilities and realise that the dream is not totally shattered. One part of the dream may not have worked out as I planned, but other fruits can grow to replace that which did not flourish. Is the glass half empty or half full? What we see in our lives has a lot to do with how we see it. My perspective will influence everything. How I think about something determines my emotions and feelings. Introverts will see life differently than extroverts. The pessimist will have a different view on life than the optimist. I often think of the saying by Henry Ford: *"Whether you think you can or think you can't — you're right."*

To help me through the pain of marriage break-up, I attended counselling. This was not easy for me because I am trained as a counsellor. It's like what they say about doctors who get sick: they are the worst patients. Here I found someone willing to listen to me, understand my troubles and who believed that I could rebuild my life again. This process allowed me to believe in myself and those around me to make life more worthwhile and to live well. I certainly recommend counselling to any person dealing with relationship problems or dealing with personal pain.

I have discovered the importance of letting go. For me letting go is a way of letting events, experiences and people 'be' as they want. There are times when we find it difficult to let go because something or someone has had a strong hold on our mind and emotions, or perhaps we have just lived a certain way for a long time. In letting go we grow and develop and come to full self-actualisation. In holding on we can become stuck and imprisoned in the past with no life or love. Yet letting go is natural to all of us. Today I let go of yesterday. I can't bring it back. Every night when I sleep I let go of the day. When I arise in the morning I let go of the night and 'I am' ready for a new day of challenges.

No man is an island and relationships are challenging. But the journey of life encourages us to reach out for intimacy with others where we can be vulnerable, real and honest. How we handle relationships — whether they work out or not — says more about us than about the other person. Always keep your dignity. Respect the other person's wishes even though that can be difficult. Each of us will go through dark tunnels in relationships and think, *"this is the end"* but remember there is always light at the end of a tunnel. You may have to sit in darkness, experience pain and go through loneliness but by staying in the moment, letting go will allow the light to shine on new beginnings.

### Laytown Beach

Darkness to
Light that was white,
Sitting on the cold,
Bold sand.

Church at back,
Awake from a nap.

Winds howl,
Seas roar,
White horses
Dance on the shore,
Sight of pure delight.

Monotonous fall
Of waves
Creating a beat,
Soothing thoughts
To repeat over and over.

Suddenly
Sun
Bursts onto stage,
Horizon
Casting light,
Its rays glow
On the seashore.

Smell the sea,
Reach the sky,
Cry if you wish,
Let your spirit fly.

This deep blue sea
Fresh and forever free
Drowns out our prison thoughts
Like the wings of a swallow.

Just salt,
Finding a smoother pebble
Or prettier shell.

Sailors,
Boats laden,
Nets untangle,
The secrets of the sea.

The gentle waves now whisper,
Enjoy simple things,
Finding joy in nature's
Treasure.

*Walking On Air* by Francis O' Toole

# 38. Brokenness

*"The worst kind of brokenness is the kind
that you don't know you have."*
— Amy Neftzger, *'The Orphanage of Miracles'.*

We all present our best self and try to carry out our daily
tasks with dignity and a smile on our faces, knowing that
life can sometimes be very difficult. I felt the pain of
brokenness when my marriage broke down. I cried daily
for one year. Then it was time to move on so I applied for
a church annulment, which took two years. This is
something I would recommend to people who have come
from a broken marriage and want peace in their faith.

When my children were sick I would gladly have
exchanged places with them to save them pain. When in
major financial difficulties I just managed to keep my
resilience alive, knowing that for one year I had only 100
euro a week to live on: I was on sick leave from work
because of a major accident. I had days with no food for
myself but always had food on the table for the children.
On many occasions when shopping my bank card was
refused because of a lack of funds. My Calvary, my pain,
my tears.

I often looked around and wondered, *"Does anyone
care?"* How could others not see my pain? I often thought
that all people in my world should be feeling sad for me
because of my brokenness. My soul was slowly leaving
my body, like the drowning man gasping for oxygen but
others marched on with their busy lives. I had to make a
choice: fight or flight. I decided to fight my darkest hours. I
decided not to be a victim of my circumstances. Then I

awoke to the reality many people experience in brokenness: their soul may be in tatters, they may be suffering because of sickness, loss, financial ruin, migration, wars, famine, bereavement but they too continue with life.

# 39. Depression

*"Depression is the inability to construct a future."*
— Rollo May.

I agree with the statement by Joyce Meyer who says, *"Depression begins with disappointment. When disappointment festers in our soul, it leads to discouragement."* I know because I went through a stage of depression. This was my experience after the breakdown of my marriage. I allowed the disappointment to overshadow everything in my life. I first tried to handle this in silence. I presented a smiling face to others but deep down my world had fallen apart; I was so disappointed. Physically I was present but in my heart and mind I was in another place. It was like a black shadow was hovering over me. This went on for three years.

Then I looked for help. First I went to my GP who placed me on medication. But I knew this was not the answer for me. I then began to talk to others in the search for answers to my problems. I was amazed by the support that was offered to me by professionals and friends. I have no doubt my depression was a result of outside influences and social pressure which were out of my control. I was lucky; I asked for help and I got a magnanimous response from others.

If you suffer from depression or know of others who do, I would say do not be afraid to admit it. Do not be afraid to ask for help.

What have I learned from my experience? Firstly, I would advise anyone who is suffering from depression not to withdraw from their social circle, whether that means family, friends or people at work. I have found that by keeping in touch with family and friends, it helped to elevate my mood.

The second thing I would say to others is face your fears. For a long time I went around in silence and even lived in denial. This was taking away my confidence and stopping me from meeting and socialising with people. The sooner you face your fear the better. The sooner you talk to others the better. Nobody can help you if they don't understand what is going on in your head.

Thirdly, I found myself comfort eating a lot. I sat and watched TV and ate unhealthy foods. The only thing I gained from this was increasing my weight. This in itself was adding to the depression. I dealt with this by letting the skill of mindfulness eating be part of my daily life. This allowed me to change my focus to healthy options when it came to food. Now I am very aware when eating foods that are bad for me. As a result of the change in focus I lost two stone weight. Not bad considering there was never a plan to lose weight.

Fourthly, I ran into problems with my sleeping habits. I often stayed up late; I was avoiding going to bed in case I would not be able to sleep. If I woke up during the night, I went to the kitchen to have a cup of tea and make a sandwich. I was eating even when I was not hungry. Then I learned to develop a bedtime routine. At night I would listen to relaxing music, as well as trying to avoid computers and social media. I would then go to bed at a set time and wake up in the morning at a set time. I was now back in control of my sleeping habits.

Fifthly, there was always the danger in finding comfort in the bottle — drink as much alcohol as possible to get rid of the problem. I now know if I had drunk more I would have avoided my emotions but this would only have made the problem worse.

Finally, I would suggest going for help if the problem continues. There are so many professional people from doctors to counsellors who are ready to help you if you suffer from depression. Above all, talk to someone. Let it be a family member or a friend. Remember: *"it's okay to have mental health issues and it's absolutely okay to look for help."*

## Depression

I am
Stuck to the bed, paralysed, unable to move.
The world passes by.
I look from a caged body shackled by the chains of a mood,
Unable to reach out, unable to cry for help,
Sinking into the dark hole.

Time passes, seconds, minutes, hours, days,
In fact they all become one.
Time stands still.
I am
alone,
My body stiff, lifeless; muscles incapable of engaging.

I am
empty but so full I cannot move,
This sack and bed become one.

Like a marble statue, no emotions or feelings.
The joy, sadness, energy, life, hurt, anger, pain
seem no more.
Where have these emotions gone that once
engaged this body
Once alive and full of zeal for life?

The shadow is cast hiding the light of day.
The gift of sight is lost; it does not want to
engage with the light.
Night becomes day, day becomes night.

Hope is lost, the fight is over.
The darkness invades.
I am
no more.

# 40. Caring for the Body

*"To keep the body in good health is a duty…otherwise we shall not be able to keep our mind strong and clear."*
— Buddha.

The body is a gift given to me by the universe. To show respect to the giver, I need to give my body the care and respect it deserves. It is important not to make too many demands on the body. It needs time to rest, relax and sleep. One day I went hiking with the Navan Trackers, a group of hill walkers. We walked the Cooley mountains, covering over fourteen kilometres. With my usual enthusiasm, I started the walk at a fast pace. Halfway up the mountain though I became very tired. My body was ready to give up. I looked at the other experienced walkers, some younger than me, some older. They all looked very relaxed. Their experience showed me that I needed to pace myself, to measure the distance, take rest and drink plenty. When I took this on board, I continued to walk and instead of setting a pace, I enjoyed the beauty of the landscape, drank cool spring water, smelled the flowers, was amazed by the panoramic view and ate some berries from the bushes that nature provided for the birds.

I realised that the walk was about enjoyment, not achievement or endurance. Even though we walked for more than five hours over rough terrain; there was no pain. The walkers were great chatters. Nature provided a feast for the eye. I even had some quiet moments alone to reflect. That day, I realised that life is like climbing a mountain. There will always be challenges, but we are all capable of reaching the mountain's peak if we care for and respect our bodies and never give up.

I am sharing this story because I know how it feels to face a huge 'mountain' or challenge and to make the decision to 'go for it'. But before you start scaling your mountain you need to be aware that, *" 'I am' a body that needs to be cared for with healthy eating, drinking, rest and sleep."* We all need to take full responsibility for the self care of our bodies. I would encourage you to be kind to yourself, and encourage yourself rather than criticising yourself. Try not to block your body with unnecessary chemicals such as smoking, too much drinking and certainly say *"no"* to drugs. I have found that having fun or being creative helped me to feel better and increase my confidence. I also found that being active helped to lift my mood, and reduced any stress or anxiety I was experiencing. Being active also gave me better physical strength and gave me more energy. I found that it is so important to find time for myself where I can relax and chill out.

I encourage you to find your own mountain in life and set your challenge. All you need is the belief that you can do it. Give it one hundred and ten per cent. Then take one step at a time.

## Celtic Warrior

We gather in pubs
For the grub,
Talk the Blarney,
Especially in Killarney.

Poems of sorrow
As if no tomorrow.
Are we glad
Just to be sad?

Sing like birds,
Dance like a social butterfly
Fluttering in the breeze.

Holy Wells,
Ringing bells,
Only in Ireland
Can you have a
Riverdance.

Men of strength,
Women of great beauty,
Priests, Poets, Parents,
Druids.

One common story,
Passion for life
As we unite.

The Celtic warrior,
Fast and furious,
Skill and speed,
Found on the hurling field.

Men are giants,
Jump ten feet tall
To grab that
Flying ball.

The Celtic warrior
Defends his land,
Trees, rivers and stone
Are his shield.

Where can you find this Celtic warrior?
In crossroads,
Byroads,
They kick against the gods,
Before the rising sun.

# 41. The Climb

*"Everything will be okay in the end. If it's not okay, then it's not the end."* — Ed Sheeran.

In an age of dwindling religious practice some traditional pilgrimages are on the increase, such as the Camino de Santiago in Spain and Croagh Patrick, the holiest mountain in Ireland. It is thought that people have been walking the Camino for more than 800 years. Watching the movie *'The Way'* featuring Martin Sheen and Emilio Estevez, I felt very moved and touched by the journey of pilgrims and how they shared their stories. The tradition of climbing Croagh Patrick stretches back over 5,000 years to the Stone Age. Pagans gathered on this mountain to celebrate the beginning of the harvest season. Croagh Patrick is now famous for its pilgrimage in honour of Ireland's patron saint, St. Patrick. It is said that the 'Reek' attracts more than one million visitors annually and thousands climb it on 'Reek Sunday', the last Sunday in July.

We can see similarities between the Camino and Croagh Patrick. Both have spectacular scenery and people journey alone or in groups. Most people make these trips for personal reasons. Some pray for a loved one. Some do it in thanksgiving. Others do it to petition, for example asking that their child do well in exams, and so on. Most people keep their intention to themselves. Each time I climbed Croagh Patrick I did it in bare feet with a good friend. The pace was slow and painful at times but rewarding when we got to the top.

I often think of this climb and apply it to the journey of life. There were times when I was on the 'Reek', I was tired and wanted to turn back. I wanted to give up. Yet I continued on the journey and I became more resilient with each step. Having a good friend is so important. We all need others to support us in our commitment and to join us in setting our goals. Being amongst friends or being in a group with people who share your beliefs offers support, fun, enjoyment and encouragement.

I invite you to take on your mountain or walk with a group of people who share a common story. It could be spiritual or just a sharing knowledge. Either way, working together will always nurture imagination, creativity and innovation.

## Friendship

A friend:
A helping hand
Embracing you as you are,
Asks no questions,
Looks for no answers,
Willing to sit with pain,
Empathise with the struggles,
No need for solutions,
Just being
Is enough.

# 42. How To Meditate

*"The future depends on what we do in the present."*
— Mahatma Gandhi.

I find meditation very relaxing and it brings harmony to my mind, body and spirit. It lowers my heart rate, reduces anxiety and stress, it deepens my feeling of well-being.

I look for a quiet place, knowing no one is going to knock on the door to disturb me. I tend to sit on the floor, perched on a cushion with my legs crossing each other and my back as straight as possible. I know that some people prefer to sit in a chair or lie comfortably on the ground. Before closing my eyes, I set my alarm clock, this could be for three or twenty minutes.

I invite you to try the techniques below.

Bring yourself into the present moment by deliberately adopting 'attentive' posture.

Then ask: what is going on with me right now? What's on my mind? How is my body? What's my energy like? How is my mood?

Notice and acknowledge your experience, instead of turning away. Accept all your experiences — thoughts, body, sensation, emotions — and for a few moments stay with whatever you find. If there are negative or positive feelings around, just let them be.

Then gently focus your full attention on the breathing. At the same time make no effort to control your breath, simply breathe naturally. Experience fully each in-breath and each out-breath as they follow one after the other. It may help in the beginning to count to seven on the in-breath and count to ten on the out-breath.

The breath can function as an anchor to keep you in the present and to maybe find some space and stillness.

Expand your awareness around the breathing to include the whole body and space it takes up — it might feel as if the whole body is breathing. Have a sense of the space around you, hold everything in awareness — how things are within you and also the world around you. Focus on your chest, shoulders, arms, legs, head and belly. Become aware of the sensation in each part of your body, don't try to change things. Whenever the mind wanders, invite the mind to come back to focus on the breath.

# 43. Having Focus

*"The real voyage of discovery consists not in seeking new landscapes, but in having new eyes."*
— Marcel Proust.

During a recent holiday with my two teenagers in sunny Spain, we decided that it was important to meet everyone's needs. On the first morning we sat at the table with pen and paper and brainstormed all our ideas, our activities, needs, our fun time and came up with a plan.

Each day began with a breakfast fit for a king with plenty of fruit, yogurt and churros covered in sugar, not forgetting toast with squashed tomatoes and plenty of virgin oil. Each of us marked our large individual bottles of water, which we had to drink by the end of the day. After clean up we headed down to the local pool, full of Spanish people basking in the sun. Here we played games, had swimming races and enjoyed the glorious sunshine.

It was important not to be out in the hot sun between 12pm and 3pm. Some days the temperatures were between 35 and 40 degrees. We had a light lunch fit for a prince, mostly fish and vegetables. Preparation of meals was difficult at times. What was best for two teenagers? My daughter, a vegetarian, did not eat meat and my son, a carnivore, did not eat vegetables. So doing the right shop was important to ensure that everyone had what his or her diet required. In the afternoon we quickly adopted the Spanish custom of having a siesta or quiet time to read, listen to music or lay down under umbrellas at the seafront.

Every second day we had a special activity: a visit to a theme park, a museum, an art gallery, music, Spanish dancing or mud baths. Whenever we had no special activity planned we stuck with the normal routine and got on our bikes in the evening, cycling three kilometres to the gym for an hour of Zumba followed by a yoga class. It was both exciting and exhausting. The sweat dripped from our bodies, but we were left with the great feeling you have after completing a wonderful workout. This was followed by a very light meal 'like a pauper', just a sandwich and drink. The carrot for the teenagers to complete the day's activities was Wi-Fi at night.

This holiday came at a good time for our family. Because of the breakdown in our marriage the children needed extra care and attention. It was also going to be different because now they were on holidays with only one parent for the first time. They needed to feel secure, knowing both parents loved and cared for them. This was a time of healing. It allowed the children and I to realise we could still be a unit. I would always tell the children that adults don't always agree. But this is not their issue or responsibility. It was for them to experience the wealth and love of both parents. They could still be children. They still had permission to love both of us, while spending time individually with us. No child should be asked to take sides when adults separate in relationships. I found the holiday a great healer for myself. It was different because we were down a very important member who always had a major part. It meant I had extra responsibility as the only adult with the children; this was not always easy. But I realised the importance of having fun and to have gratitude for the very simple things in life.

There is no doubt that exercise like dancing, yoga, cycling, walking or swimming bring freedom to the body and opens energy waves. If we are flexible, we will be able to blend with the challenges life will present. I know myself that getting older gracefully means that exercise is important to maintain flexibility. A healthy body renews my mind and deepens wisdom, knowledge and love. It has helped me to be open to the many changes and challenges that I have encountered over the last number of years. Having focus gave us a wonderful time.

# 44. Music

*"Then I'll stand on the ocean until I start sinking."*
— Bob Dylan.

Listening to music is a tremendous way to escape from the world of pressure and anxiety. Music has an amazing ability to reach into our being and demand an emotional response. This response may become a choice in how we wish to express ourselves externally. Research confirms that emotion plays an important role in our motives for listening to music. For example, listening to classical music can help us to be calm; listening to loud aggressive music can stir up our emotions in preparation for a battle; romantic music can help loving relationships and so on.

Throughout the ages, music was used to call out to the masses. For example, we know that the sound of the drum was used on many occasions to summon men to fight in battle. This same sound is used in a ritualistic way by some tribal cultures to stimulate the sex drive. It can be used in a solemn way in the cathedral to call us to offer worship to the Creator. Maybe our connection with the drum is a strong reminder of our heart beating to the heartbeat of our mother when we were in the safety of the womb. The sound of drums has many different meanings for different people.

Today music is used in many different ways. Rock bands are often seen to represent chaos and the anti-establishment. Liturgical music is used in churches to help raise the emotions in prayer. In dance clubs, music is used to call individuals to freedom of expression or to set a romantic theme that stimulates the sexual drive.

Hence, choosing the right kind of music is important when caring for our souls. I regularly listen to music by the famous composer Beethoven, who was born in 1769 and raised in the city of Bonn, the city on the Rhine. On a recent school tour I visited the home of his birthplace. I then went into the local Jesuit church for a moment of reflection. I was impressed to think the Jesuits were playing Beethoven's music in the background. In my experience a symphony orchestra creates the sound of the Divine. If I want to go into a place of calm and be free of anxiety, then I find that gentle classical music is best suited. While I hear it with my ears it's quite incredible how it passes through my body and touches my soul in a unique way more than any other kinds of music, allowing for peace and stress-free moments. While listening to classical music the mind transcends the soul, awakening a new flow of energy. The body, mind and soul become one unit. In this new state of total relaxation the mind is relaxed and open to creativity.

Music is also a universal language of healing that can do so much to help people believe in themselves. Along with my teenage daughter Zoe, I watched the Ariana Grande 'One Love' concert on television as she returned to the stage in Manchester two weeks after a suicide bombing killed 22 victims at her concert in the city. The music was upbeat and full of motivation, moving the audience who cheered loudly and shed tears at the same time for those who died. Both myself and my daughter were teary-eyed and emotional as she performed 'Be Alright' and 'Break Free'. She shouted, *"Manchester, we're gonna be alright"*. I was so moved by this young lady and what she achieved. I salute her and all the many talented famous musicians who performed that night. They raised millions of pounds to support the families of the bombing victims and have given hope to so many. I loved the moment when Justin Bieber said, *"The only way to fight evil is to fight evil with love."*

*Walking On Air* by Francis O' Toole

# 45. Chess

*"The beauty of a move lies not in its appearance but in the thought behind it."* — Aron Nimzowitsch.

One of the first board games I ever played was the game of chess. This is such a wonderful game that it should be taught to every student at home or in school. It is said that the game of chess goes back 1,500 years and originated in India (some historians believe the game originated in China). The game spread from India to Persia. When the Arabs conquered Persia, the Muslim world enjoyed chess and brought it into southern Europe. The game of chess always had its own artistic expression and was played by those who wanted to use the power of the mind to out-do their opponents. This continues today.

A German study indicated that while testing experts in the game of chess, both sides of the brain were active. It also suggested that one's IQ develops after playing chess for four months. I introduced each of my children to the game of chess at a young age. I certainly believe that many skills can be developed through this game, especially the skills of creativity, logical thinking, critical thinking, problem solving and independent decision-making. What a great way to build up resilience in young people, to help them believe in themselves and take responsibility when they make a false move.

Of course now that I am over 53 years of age, I want to keep the brain active, doing what I call 'brain workouts' by playing chess or reading. If we keep the brain active it will help to keep Alzheimers and dementia at bay. I often wonder why chess is not introduced into schools as part of the curriculum? Above all, chess helps to increase problem-solving skills. It helps to improve memory since so many rules and moves need to be remembered. I have found that in a chess match, one has to think fast to solve problems because your opponent is constantly changing the parameters.

For three years, I held a men's shed in my house. Each week eight men called to play chess. There was very little conversation, mostly silence. Focus on the game was the thing. Some games went on for hours and were continued the following week. This proves that playing chess can stimulate deep concentration and calm, helping to centre and relax players, especially if they are experiencing degrees of stress or anxiety. The great thing about chess is that every game is different and every opponent you meet will have his or her own style, making each game unique, unpredictable and challenging. Once the game begins there are thousands of moves each opponent can consider so chess offers a true competition with infinite parameters. When you win you'll have won fair and square without question. There is no room for cheating; when you win, it's a great confidence booster. Your move!

# 46. Sailing

*"Creativity is just connecting things. When you ask creative people how they did something, they feel a little guilty because they didn't really do it, they just saw something. It seemed obvious to them after a while. That's because they were able to connect experiences they've had and synthesize new things."* — Steve Jobs.

Neuroplasticity is a scientific term referring to the mind's ability to learn new skills. The brain consists of many channels, a bit like a maze. If I take on a new challenge, I create a new channel in my brain, but in order for me to become skilled and for this new 'channel' to remain, I need to practise, practise and practise. When we repeat and practise constantly we no longer have to think about a movement or an action, it becomes part of our existence. 'I am' what I set out to achieve.

The key to creating a new channel is getting the brain to believe, *"I need to do this"* and repeating the new practice over and over again. I believe that we can learn any new thing with thirty days of repeated practice.

When I celebrated my 50th birthday I wanted to take on a new challenge. I had the opportunity to work as a deckhand on a tall ship, the sailing vessel *Irene* for five weeks.

On day one I hadn't a clue what to do. I was unable to keep my balance as the tall ship sailed on the Irish Sea both day and night. My stomach began to show weakness, my mind began telling me that I was in the wrong place. Yet I was out on the open sea with a crew of four: the captain, first mate, cook and deckhand. For the ship to sail successfully and for health and safety reasons, every person counted, including me. Despite my fears I made a conscious choice to get fully stuck into my work and to learn as much as I could.

When I had fears I had to face them and do the required work anyway. The success of the journey depended on individual actions that we had to repeat daily. As the sails blended with the wind I too blended with every activity. I left my own learning style behind and took a new approach to everything. Gradually I lost my fear. Before I knew it my body and hands were repeating the same gestures daily. Putting up the sails demanded all of our energy and physical strength. Usually six people would carry out this task but that was a luxury we didn't have. It was essential that we teamed up in pairs to do everything. We had to develop the daily skill of letting up and bringing down ten sails, depending on how demanding the winds were.

My favourite part of the journey was the time spent at the wheel of this mighty sailing ship with the captain while he kept watch. The watch hours were from midnight till four in the morning, then eight o'clock to noon and finally four o'clock to eight at night. The most precious moments for me were at night. After checking the maps and setting the compass to point in the direction of our course, we were ready to sail into the night. I had never been on a sailing ship before and now I was sailing for twenty-four hours a day on the seas from Drogheda port to the Isle of Man to Scotland, past Wales and down the English Channel. Looking at the compass and watching the bright stars at night to guide us was a magnificent experience. Yes, I felt like the explorers of old, such as Christopher Columbus.

During the day when the repeated daily rituals were complete, I had the opportunity to watch whales floating like gentle giants. Not far behind them basking sharks could be clearly seen seeking new prey. Whenever I saw birds nearby I knew land was not far away.

'I am' a sailor, fulfilling daily duties, working ropes and learning about knots, learning about compasses and map reading, learning constantly through my daily duties, appreciating nature, facing my fears. As the captain wrote daily in his logbook, I too spent time writing about my experience in my personal journal. I had transformed my intention to learn new things into actions. Neuroplasticity had created new channels in my brain. I had learned so much in such a short time. I had refused to be paralysed by fear and had taken responsibility for my choice to be on that ship. If I found an activity difficult, I worked on it until I could perform it without thinking.

When you take on new projects, I encourage you to let go of your fear, learn through repeated daily actions and then review your work after thirty days and see what you have discovered. *"Do not be afraid"* (Matthew 14:27), set your sails, blend with the wind, be inspired and discover new horizons.

# 47. My Awakening

*"Life is a journey, not a destination."*
— Ralph Waldo Emerson.

In June 2015 I planned to sea-kayak up the east coast of Ireland and down the Wild Atlantic Way. My excitement grew as I planned the journey from Laytown in County Meath to Donegal. I knew that this trip was going to be special and I wanted the adventure to be fun and a lifelong memory. At one stage I headed out to Gola Island off Donegal, or in Gaelic 'Gabhla', which is less than two kilometres in a kayak from Gaoth Dobhair on the mainland. There are lots of cottages and minor roads on Gola but very little transport. Although stone cottages still stand, the last of the inhabitants left for the mainland in the 1960s. On that day as I strolled and chatted with people, I discovered that a number of people move to Gola for the summer.

I encountered artists, birdwatchers, photographers, walkers and rock climbers. Their main pastime was chatting to every person they met. Nobody rushed. There was plenty of time to engage and connect with other people. In one day you could easily conquer all of Gola Island.

Our busy lives mean that we're always in danger of missing opportunities. Few of us are really in the present moment; instead we're miles away in our heads. We're thinking about yesterday's events or planning tomorrow's. Instead of being really present, we're really absent. We all have an inbuilt 'auto-pilot' and this has many advantages. Imagine what it would be like if you had to learn how to cycle every time you got on a bicycle or what it would be like if you had to learn to drive from scratch every time you got into a car? So it's useful to be able to do things naturally and we take this for granted. However, if we're always on automatic pilot we're not experiencing the real moment. I would prefer to be fully alive and engaged with life rather than do things automatically. There will be many times when we will make mistakes but if we learn from them, then the mistakes were valuable experiences. My recent encounter with 'my freak wave' was a valuable experience but unfortunately painful.

As the summer ended I landed on a beautiful beach near Bundoran. There were plenty of wild waves in the sea. The perfect storm was calling for any surfer. They say that if it's in your blood to dance, nobody is going to stop you. Once you venture near the sea, safety is primary. Well, kayaking, tall ships or swimming in the sea and surfing are not pastimes for couch potatoes. They are demanding and they take place in an ever-changing, often unpredictable environment. I was fortunate enough to train as a lifeguard with some experienced instructors at the Garda College, Templemore. I'm aware of the dangers of water and the importance of ocean safety. In saying that, on this particular day I ignored some of the most important ocean rules.

A friend who was an experienced surfer had lent me a very large, fibreglass surfboard. As it turns out, there was an orange weather alert that day and, really, nobody should have been in the sea. I knew I could not go out in the kayak but in my enthusiasm to get out in the surf, I foolishly thought I could head out to sea on a surfboard … a small wave can pack quite a punch. One cubic foot of water weighs about 62 pounds. That means a cubic yard of water weighs about 1,684 pounds. That's almost one tonne! Water isn't solid but it's pretty heavy and can knock you around quite a bit as I learned first-hand when a freak wave knocked me off my board head first into the water with no idea where my board was. The waves pummelled me into the ocean floor, turned me upside-down and my body was WHACKed and THUMPed repeatedly as though I was in a boxing ring with a world heavyweight champion.

I think I was caught in a rip current and as I struggled to come up for air, BANG! My surfboard slammed into my head. I experienced an extremely bright light but no pain; in fact, I felt very calm, even relaxed. It was as if my full body and mind were at one with the ocean waves. I was full of unusual feelings. I felt a warm glow, extreme peace, no pain, I even felt fulfilled. Somewhere in this deep blue sea, a light was shining on me. Suddenly I was jolted from this calm, relaxed place to a place of horror. I gasped for air, spitting water from my mouth and lungs. I felt the urgency to survive. I could spot land. I kept my focus on one point and somehow struggled back to shore.

The rest is history. Lifeguards came to the rescue and an ambulance took me to Sligo General Hospital. I knew my face was a mess but I still felt calm and peaceful. I was really glad to be alive. It was incredible having a near-death experience; all the amazing thoughts that went through my mind: thinking of family, friends, children, things still to do. As it turned out, I had lost seven teeth; I had to have three other teeth reconstructed to save the structure of my mouth. I had to have three operations involving bone grafting and four pins being installed in my jaw.

In hindsight I now know that the whole experience was my awakening. A freak wave may have caused my accident, but ultimately I view it as a 'shot in the mouth' from God. The message was to live life 110%. I was angry with God for years. I have a very strong faith but I really believed that God had abandoned me because I chose to leave the priesthood for a different calling. My marriage did not go to plan. I had a very sick child for years and financial pressure kicked in with the death of the Celtic Tiger in Ireland. Many negative thoughts came my way. So part of me gave up. I was just 'surviving', sleepwalking through life and feeling very much a victim of circumstances. I blamed God. My world was covered with a shadow. After the freak wave though, everything changed. Now I live not for today or tomorrow or next week. I live every second, in the moment, here and now.

The bright light I saw that day continues with me today. I no longer see the world as Plato described. I no longer watch shadows on the wall of a cave. I now see all things more clearly than ever before, with this extra bright light shining daily for me. I experience a new brightness, a beauty full of colour, all inspiring. This light is everywhere; I see the world with all its richness and the joy and love of people. I see beauty in everything from the weeds in the ground to the people I love and meet in my daily life. The light in my life is finally switched 'on'. I had a lot of time off work as a result of my injuries; plenty of time for reflection. I now see life and the people around me in a totally positive way and I'm always reminded that it was not my turn to meet the Creator.

Since my 'awakening' I now take a more radical approach to my everyday experience. I begin my day with 20 minutes of meditation, followed by 20 minutes of yoga. I have learned that life is difficult but there is always someone else who has a more disastrous story than you. So don't get caught up with the small stuff. Start your day with a positive attitude, identify one thing that you are grateful for, don't get caught up in the negatives and reduce the time you spend with negative people. Use positive statements, like the following:

- I draw good things into my life;
- I attract abundance;
- I have amazing strength within me;
- Beautiful things are coming into my life;
- I love and approve of myself;
- I am not my past; I am creating my own future;
- I expect good health;
- I am gifted;
- I feel comfort growing daily;
- I acknowledge my own self worth;
- Comfort, healing, hope, health, abundance, happiness are all coming my way;
- I am flourishing.

Write down the above statements and place them into your journal. Consider all experiences — irrespective of how they first appear — as 'win-win'.

*Walking On Air* by Francis O' Toole

# 48. Fully Awake

*"What counts is not the enormity of the task, but the size of the courage."* — Matthieu Ricard.

From school to college to the university of life, I have often spent much time daydreaming. Thinking about times in the past or thinking about times in the future. I often wonder how many of us are fully active and fully alive in any one moment in life. We may do all the right things in life: go to school, go to college, get a job, develop our careers and take on the commitments of relationships and children. All highly commendable but how many of us allow our boats to be rocked? How many of us like security and refuse to be open to taking risks? How many of us will go against the tide and be leaders of justice, fight for what is right, speak out against bullying, give real example in the workplace? How many of us are willing to disturb the peace, to be prophets, to be willing to take on the challenge of making the world a better place?

The disruptor is like the wave of an ocean crashing against the rocks. The psychologist Maslow speaks of human needs: food, shelter, water, security, money and acceptance but very few reach the top of the pyramid of which he speaks when we reach self-actualisation. These people are the ones who disturb the peace, have hearts full of passion. Not only do they look outwards and dream of a better world, they also dig deep, finding vision within to create a better world.

# 49. The Salmon of Knowledge

*"To meditate is to listen with a receptive heart."*
— Shakyamuni Buddha.

There is a lovely old Celtic story told in Slane about Fionn MacCumhaill, the greatest leader of the Fianna in Ireland. In his youth, Fionn was sent to live with an old wise man Finnegas, a poet who lived on the banks of the Boyne. He was known all over Ireland for his wisdom and knowledge. In ancient Ireland a poet was a very special person. They had skills no one else had. They had knowledge about the ways of the world and knowledge about nature, birds, bees, animals, etc. Fionn would sit by the fire daily and listen to the stories of the old wise man. Fionn was always asking questions and one day he asked the poet if there was anything he did not know. It was then that the poet told Fionn about the Salmon of Knowledge. It is said because he had eaten all the nuts from the hazel trees that the salmon was full of knowledge. He told Fionn that he lived on the edge of the river for years in the hope of catching the Salmon of Knowledge. Then whoever caught the salmon and ate it would become the wisest person in the land, receiving many gifts, talents and powers.

It happened that one day the druid caught the Salmon of Knowledge. He could not curtail his excitement telling Fionn of this great catch. The first thing they both did was to start a fire and put a spit on it to cook the salmon. The salmon had to be turned over regularly, so it would not burn. As the fire was burning low, it was in danger of going out. The druid rushed to get more firewood and left his protégé Fionn to care for the salmon. Young Fionn did as he was told but saw the salmon was burning on one side. A blister appeared. In fright he decided to burst the blister with his finger, but burned his finger in the process. Finally he placed his finger in his mouth to ease the burning pain, not noticing that some skin of the salmon was on his finger. As soon as he tasted it he became the wisest person in the land, with extra gifts, powers and tremendous ability in poetry. When Finnegas came back with the wood, he knew from Fionn's glowing eyes what had happened. I have no doubt that Finnegas was sad to be glad because now this young man had acquired the many gifts life has to offer. His prodigy was ready to leave and become a great leader.

I often say to students in school, *"Life is simple, don't complicate it."* After working in the caring profession since 1988 as a psychotherapist and guidance counsellor, I believe that much can be achieved through meditation and creating full awareness of our human needs.

It's especially important for young people to grow and develop to have at least one significant adult in their life that they can depend on. Young people need adults whom they can trust to talk to and to gain wisdom from. A good friend of mine often said, *"Anything can be talked about."* Today young people are caught up with so many distractions, social media, peer pressure, exam pressure, etc. This list is endless.

I believe that meditation and mindfulness can help to address some of the more common problems in our busy lives. Over the years as a therapist, clients have shared with me issues ranging from stress, tiredness, burnout, physical aches and pain, anxiety and depression.

How we choose to deal with pressure is our choice. But a problem shared is a problem half solved. Mindfulness and meditation will also have a positive impact on the life of young people if given time. It will help them to de-stress, to find their own unique space of calm and to be ready for whatever challenges (good or bad) their busy life will bring them. We all have a rich pool of strength deep within us. We need to tap into this amazing resource. Be open to change and, strangely, remember that change brings stress. By practising daily meditation and mindfulness your life will change. It has changed mine for the better. This life-changing practice will empower you to manage your stress at home and at work with much more ease and efficiency.

I will be bold enough to point out some of the changes you can expect if you practise meditation and mindfulness regularly: improved motivation and energy levels; better performance in study; improved cognitive ability; more feelings of happiness and contentment; improved productivity and efficiency; improved immune system and general health; improved memory and concentration and increased brainwave activity; enhanced communication and creativity; better ability to deal with loss, bereavement, separation, divorce, comfort eating, overindulgence in alcohol or drugs; and, overall, increased resilience in the face of inevitable daily stress.

It is important for all of us to develop skills in the practice of meditation and mindfulness. Daily, we will notice it working. I suggest that you keep a journal, write your daily reflections in it and see what insights you gain. Creating awareness in the present moment will reduce stress. The more mindfulness and meditation you practise, the more you will feel the benefit. Start today.

I have developed my own personal plan to help me deal with stress. Daily, I ask myself the question, *"On a scale of one to ten, where is my stress level?"* Point 1 on the scale means no stress and point 10 on the scale indicates high levels of stress. Once I go over point 5, I know that it is important to build in structures to help me reduce that stress level. Through meditation and mindfulness I have developed the following plan for myself to provide a balance between mind, body and spirit. Once the balance is there, I live with no stress. If the balance is not there, then my stress levels creep up. Try the following and see how it will reduce your stress levels.

Body: daily practice — yoga, running, healthy eating, focus on nature, smile, cycling, focus on the breath and body scan.

Mind: journal writing, reading, poetry, social media, communication, inspirational reading, gratitude, intention seeking.

Spirit: meditation, mindfulness, reflection, prayer, visualisation, body scan, music, dance, shows, travel, family, love, laughter, creativity, dream the impossible.

The above may seem complicated but it is rather simple. I practice the 20:20:20 rule daily: 20 minutes of exercise, 20 minutes of meditation and 20 minutes of journaling.

By practising the above, you will open up the energy flow in your body, release the power within and dramatically reduce stress. Once you have developed your energy flow, you will progress to a more powerful way of living and connect with the Divine energy flow.

This Divine energy flow is so powerful, that it will allow you to change the world around you, touching off the impossible.

## Slane Bridge

Down by Slane Bridge
The Boyne rushed up to the ridge.
I brought my bright-eyed lover
Under the trees' cover.

The waters flowed with mighty power.
My emotions stirred with powerful passion.
We gazed at the falling stars
While listening to the ripples of the Boyne.

As I ponder on the bend of the Boyne,
I could feel the curves of her body,
The wild water flow,
The gentle hair glow.

I hear the cuckoo,
The crows fluttered near,
But I was not afraid
As I danced with my dear.

In the stillness of the night
Silence eased across the land.
All was peaceful, all was quiet
As I held my lover's hand.

*Walking On Air* by Francis O' Toole

# 50. Taking A Break

*"To many people holidays are not voyages of discovery, but a ritual of reassurance."* — Philip Andrew Adams.

When on holidays abroad I give myself permission to taste as many different foods as possible. I often choose the 'menu of the day' that's on offer and — though not usually too exciting — the meals are generally cheap and come with bread, water and a beer, free of charge. Great value! If I'm near the sea I might have seafood and rice, or sometimes I have tapas, snacks designed to be served with drinks. On holidays I often use the mantra, now 'I am' off duty so it's okay to chill out. I tend to eat and drink more than usual especially when the cost of food and drink is so much cheaper than Ireland. I feel the need to nourish my body with food, drink and plenty of rest. Everything slows down and nobody rushes anywhere.

There is huge scientific evidence to prove that not eating the right foods or eating too quickly and not allowing food to digest properly can lead to lots of health problems, such as obesity and heart problems. The good news is that we can all break old habits and create new habits, especially when it comes to eating.

I am reminded of the Buddhist practice to eat mindfully. The next time you are having a meal, ask yourself if you are eating mindfully. Are you with the people you care about? Are meals used as a time of rest and renewal? Do you have the time to sit, rest and really enjoy your food? Or are you too busy to taste the food?

When I made a choice to become aware of my eating habits and to eat mindfully, I stopped overeating. Now I eat less, I take my time enjoying my food and I put time into my shopping to ensure that I find the right foods. I unintentionally lost two stone in weight and I still really enjoy my food. My overall well-being increased, my mind has improved and I now have the capability and energy to take on a regular exercise routine.

The following are some tips on mindful eating. I practise them and invite you to try them out.

(1) I try to take my time when eating, chew my food for longer. This will mean that I will need to eat less and my brain will send my body the message that I am full.

(2) I often try eating food with my non-dominant hand. Yes, we were all trained to eat with our knife and fork but maybe this habit needs to change because it's encouraging us to eat more!

(3) The last time I was in a Chinese restaurant, I really enjoyed trying to master the chopsticks. It certainly slowed me down; I was not able to rush my food. Why not try this with some meals at home!

(4) I often try to eat my meal with my eyes closed. This helps me to really smell the food and enjoy the taste. Mind you, this can be messy; best tried in the comfort of your home.

(5) I often try cooking different types of food: non-traditional and from other cultures. This can be great fun. It also means that I need to have my shopping list prepared before I go to the local store. If you try this, it will enhance your creativity and imagination.

(6) Sometimes I enjoy eating in silence and 'I am' careful not to rush my food when eating alone. Sharing food with others lends a sense of occasion. I often invite a discussion on mindful eating with my family or friends or those who I share my meals with. I ask them for suggestions. Setting the table is one of the things I trained my children to do at an early age. This gave them the belief that mealtimes were special. It was a time to share, laugh and have fun. They talked about their school day and I might share a little about my work. As they got older the conversations changed to relationships, politics, religion and the sharing of ideas.

(7) Whenever I gather for a special meal of celebration, I always ask am I eating mindfully? Am I really enjoying and appreciating the food, especially if someone else prepared it? When we eat with other people, it is more than a meal. Eating in the company of others helps us to relax, care, share, nourish, tell stories and talk about challenges.

(8) I have often introduced special theme nights when cooking at home: this adds a bit of fun. It reminds me of different trips we have taken and it changes our cooking routine. Friday night could be Italian, Saturday night could be African, and so on.

Break the old habits, create new habits and eat mindfully. Watch how your body and mind develop as a result. You will become a physically-fit human being, ready for the challenges the world presents to you.

## O'Connell Bridge, Dublin

O'Connell Bridge,
Full of life, full of buzz,
On a quest,
Do not guess,
Be full of zest.

O'Connell Bridge,
The lamps'
Golden glow
Seen even in the snow
Right up to the GPO.

O'Connell Bridge,
Locks attached,
Lovers cuddle
From the cold,
The old man sings.

O'Connell Bridge,
Romantic melodies.
The boy with the flute
Looks like a duke.
Sends shivers up the Liffey.

O'Connell Bridge,
Beggars with empty cups
Raise their hand,
No words spoken,
Tokens shaken.

# 51. Light

*"We can easily forgive a child who is afraid of
the dark; the real tragedy of life is when men
are afraid of the light."* — Plato.

I think that all Irish people or those looking for a sense of
the spirit of their ancestors should at some stage visit
Newgrange, Knowth and Dowth. Newgrange is a passage
tomb in the Boyne Valley, County Meath which is more
than 5,500 years old. This passage tomb was built by Stone
Age farmers to celebrate the light. The passage and main
chamber were constructed so that they would align with
the rising sun at the winter solstice. Newgrange may be
seen as an ancient temple where spiritual and religious
ceremonies took place to worship the light and to bury the
dead. I hope they will pass from this world of darkness to
the eternal world of light.

It's incredible to think that before organised religion ever
came to Ireland, the native people had the wisdom to
search for meaning and discovered something special in
celebrating the light more than 5,000 years ago. What
happens when the sun rises to give light to the world? The
shadows of blackness across the land hiding all in their
path are cast to one side by the light. The light allows the
world to be seen in all its beauty and majesty. The light
allows plants and trees to express their magnificence, their
colours bright and dull. The light allows animals, man and
woman to engage in this awesome world.

If only we could allow the light to envelop our bodies and
souls. We would then become a beacon of hope to the lost
world we live in with so many conflicts and wars. We would

all shine in personality, have real depth, wisdom and light. We would be as a lighthouse guiding ships in the darkness of night.

Maybe we need to make a real decision about the light which is the grace of God becoming part of our lives. When we allow the light to shine within, only then will we be able to show joy to the outside world. If we allow the light in we will create a whole new value system, deepen our awareness and develop our vision. Through the light we will see the beauty and perfection of others. We will no longer strive for grief with our enemies. The light will allow all of us to overcome the darkness, to be forgiving and understanding. The light will want us to seek realness, peace, love and kindness. The light will allow us to love and accept ourselves as we are: body, mind and soul.

By connecting with the light, we allow one another to connect with other humans and with all living beings, animals and plants. Connecting with the light will change our relationships and attitude towards those who have gone before us. Through the light we will create a ritual of respect and honour, linking us to the past and allowing it to shape our future, enriching our present. It is only by accepting and honouring our ancestors we can further understand who we are, where we came from and then with courage embark on our journey as a leading light.

## Graveside

Bitter tears flow,
Cascading down my cheeks,
Like vinegar on his side.
Why me?

Empty.
Lost.
Cries of pain.
All in vain.

Oh God,
You abandoned your Son,
Took my love,
Leaving me in pain.

Alone.
Headstone carved.
Weeping as a wave
Crashing on dry land.

# 52. The Power of Stones in Irish Life

*"I see his face in every flower;*
*The thunder and the singing of the birds*
*Are but his voice — and carven by his power*
*Rocks are his written words."*

These lines are taken from the poem *'I See His Blood Upon The Rose'* written by Joseph Mary Plunkett, who was executed in 1916 during the Easter Rising. In the poem he speaks of his passion and belief in the Christian faith. The poem tells us about finding the Divine in the world we live in and that God's word will never be forgotten as long as rocks remain. The stones are a reminder of the solid presence of God in the awesome world of nature. The poem acknowledges the pain and suffering in life, but when we sacrifice our life for the greater good of others, we achieve life's highest goal in the same way that Christ suffered on the cross for the good of humanity. The poem challenges us to move beyond ourselves and find meaning in something greater, whether it is service to our community or a higher power.

If you ever travel to Blarney Castle, Blarney, County Cork and climb to the top of the castle you will find the famous 'Stone of Eloquence' which is better known as the 'Blarney Stone'. You will be invited to hang upside-down over a sheer drop and kiss the stone, which is said to give the gift of eloquence. You will hear different legends about the origins of the stone but some say that it is the Lia Fáil, a magical stone upon which Irish kings were crowned and anointed.

In Kerry we have the Skellig Islands, called Na Scealaga in Gaelic. The islands are two small, steep and rocky islands lying about ten miles west of Bolus Head on the Iveragh Peninsula in County Kerry. They are famous for their thriving wild bird populations, including gannets and puffins, and also for an early Christian monastery that is now a world heritage site. They are symbols of the faith of early Christians who braved and survived the harshest of conditions on the edge of the known world. Don't forget the latest Star Wars movie contains scenes which were shot here!

Every part of Ireland has places and fields of stone from the Cliffs of Moher to the Devil's Bit in Templemore, County Tipperary to the mountain of Ben Bulben in Sligo, at the base of which William Butler Yeats is buried.

Folklore, legend and fact have given us many stories about stones and the messages they can reveal. Often these stories have shaped the beliefs of local people.

This summer I encountered three people who handed me the gift of a stone.

The first stone I received is called a 'hag stone' and it was given to be me by a white witch. There are many in Ireland who continue to believe in White Witchcraft, a faith built around a spirituality of nature. I would describe it as a peaceful faith that is deeply connected to nature and is unattached to material wealth. This 'witchcraft' has its roots in ancient pagan Ireland that worshipped the power and energy of nature. Our pagan ancestors had a great understanding of the healing properties of herbs and oils. Often in country houses you may notice a small stone with holes in it placed on a window ledge or with a bunch of keys tied to it. These are known as 'hag stones' and their origins date back to the time when witches rode along the hedgerows at night. The stones were kept as a form of protection, whether as protection from black magic, destructive natural forces or even nightmares. It was said that for those with the third eye looking through the stone, it was a portal between two worlds: good and evil.

The white witches I have met talk of love and peace, of the energy we receive from nature and they give praise and honour to the earth, the sun and the moon, which they regard as 'One'. Regardless of our beliefs, we could learn a lot from the way in which those who practise White Witchcraft care and protect the environment.

At one time people believed that a local witch could cast evil spells that would destroy livestock, stop cows giving milk and stop hens laying eggs. On many occasions as a priest in late 1980s and early 1990s, I was called out to a local farm to bless the animals and land so that they would prosper. I too was used to cast a spell, to call on the Divine for protection. Did you know that every altar in a church has a special stone, a Holy Stone? In it are relics of saints of the church.

The second stone I received was a crystal. A psychic gave it to me. This person believed that I had gone through a lot of suffering and needed a protective 'shield' of some sort to protect me and to allow the white light to shine. I was happy to receive the crystal stone. It is just an ordinary stone but it's very clear — almost see-through — and rugged at the edges. The psychic said that the stone would protect me from outside dangers. She also said, *"As you wake up each morning, use your imagination to create an invisible cloak and then place it around you. It will protect you with white light that will outdo the darkness."*

The third stone is the touchstone I wear on my finger. Historically a 'touch stone' was a hard black stone, such as jasper or basalt, and it was used to test the quality of gold or silver. The gold or silver was drawn across the stone and the streak the metal left on the stone was compared with that of a standard alloy. However, I came across another definition of 'touchstone' which I prefer: *"An excellent quality or example that is used to test the excellence or genuineness of others."* I wear a gold ring with a simple blue stone as a symbol of God's love and calling. To me it means: *"Do not be afraid, God is with you"*. These words are written three hundred and sixty-five times in the Bible, once for each day of the year.

God is with you.

# 53. The Truth Will Set You Free — John 8:32

*"No one is more hated than he who speaks the truth."* —
Plato.

Her Excellency Mary Robinson, President of Ireland, in her inaugural speech in Dublin Castle, December 3, 1990 referred to the old concept of the 'Fifth Province', expressing this emerging Ireland of tolerance and empathy. She goes on to say the old Irish province is coicead, meaning a 'fifth' and yet we all know there are only four geographical provinces on this island. So where is the 'fifth'? The 'Fifth Province' is not anywhere here or there, north or south, east or west. It is a place within each of us. That place that is open to the other; the swinging door which allows us to venture out and others to venture in.

We have Leinster in the east, Munster in the southwest, Connacht in the west and Ulster in the north. While Tara, County Meath, was the political centre of Ireland, tradition has it that this 'Fifth Province' acted as a second centre, a necessary balance. Mary Robinson described herself as recognising a new Ireland where she would become a symbol of reconciliation and healing; a 'Fifth Province'.

The greatest danger is that we tend to place a wall between our visions and ourselves. I call this wall 'the wall of fear'. As a psychotherapist I have listened to people share their life stories for over twenty years and I have found that fear is their greatest obstacle. People have often shared that as a child or in school, someone or an event created fear. Now even as adults, they allow the triggers of fear to hold them back. Of course this is a learned behaviour, a habit created over many years. I always try to get people to break their old habits and create new ones. Creating new habits with no walls of fear holding them back is challenging. How many of us are caught up in guilt or shame that prevents us from trying new projects? Or how many of us may be afraid of failure and what others may think?

The truth will set you free. I admit that I have fears and feelings of guilt and shame. I admit that I am afraid of failure or being rejected. It is important to create awareness of our feelings and emotions. If we can do this, we can build ways of overcoming the obstacles and moving on. We need to embrace our weaknesses; this will allow us to build on our strengths. As the saying goes: *"Feel the fear and do it anyway."*

To help us to find our true meaning, we need to be truthful with ourselves. We need to embrace the person that we are. We all have the ability to celebrate who we are as a person. We don't have to change to meet the needs of others. I am free if I can accept the person that I am, unique, special, full of ability, talent and skill. Regardless of my age, whether I'm 12 or 92, I need to build on my strengths and create awareness of who I am as a person.

My greatest fear was to be asked to speak in public. When I look back on my school days, I was quiet, shy and reserved, especially in primary school. I would have been best described as an introvert. At that time, I considered this to be a negative thing. I did everything to distract the teacher from asking me to read out loud in class. It was a common practice for the teacher to read from the text book and then get the students to follow wherever he/she had left off. I dreaded the word *"next"* knowing it was getting closer to me and it would be my turn to read out loud in class. My heart would jump from sixty-five beats per minute to one hundred and twenty beats per minute. My forehead and hands would be full of perspiration, my mind racing away with itself in panic. My fear was causing havoc in my life. For a while I never really understood what I was afraid of. Then I had to try to identify my fear and be very specific about it. I had to define what was happening to me and what was causing my fear. When I acknowledged my fear I was able to work on it, first by speaking in public where I felt I was secure and there would be no judgement. Gradually my confidence began to grow. It is amazing to think that later in life I would choose professions which demanded I would be confident at public speaking. My greatest weakness became my greatest strength.

I recommend we all ask ourselves the deep philosophical questions. *"Who am I? Why was I born? What is the purpose of my Being?"* Most of us shy away from asking such philosophical questions. We may think they are too abstract. We find it easier to get caught up in the latest celebrity scandal. If I am being honest, could I stand up right now and give a full account of the person I am? I am capable of reflecting on my life. I believe that we all need to develop a dream, a vision or a mission in life if we are to have peace of mind or heart. Many of us will place this dream and vision in our working careers, believing that a successful career is most important.

Success is good. Real success is not based on how much money we earn or how much material wealth we gather in our lifetime. We are truly wealthy when we allow ourselves to be real, when we allow our souls to become fully alive and free to dance with the rhythm of life. This is achieved by being totally honest with ourselves. We need to nourish the soul through meditation, reflection, reading inspirational books, gathering information with critical thinking, knowing the difference between the objective and subjective; we must be always willing to listen to a wise and experienced person.

The soul will allow us to grow and develop naturally if I am willing to allow this to happen. The challenge is to become a reflective person, to understand who 'I am', my purpose in life, and my role in the wider community, understanding my emotions and feelings. The human being is so complex unlike any other animal or particle from nature. The human being is the only living being that can decide with rational thought how to live his/her life. The human being is capable of great things, great imagination. If we are true to ourselves life will be full of beauty, joy, fulfilment, success and richness beyond our imagination. The soul is capable of giving us so much wealth but we need to acknowledge this.

I believe that we are all destined to have a dream and vision that will marry with our values and belief systems. We are all gifted people with lots of talents and abilities, but we need to discover what they are. Was it Socrates who said that the unexamined life is not worth living?

When we allow for this growth, great things will happen as we journey through life. We will go beyond surviving. We will discover the secret of success, ask philosophical questions, develop dreams and visions. We will live an extraordinary life knowing that the truth has set us free. We will be living the 'Fifth Province', finding new direction as we journey through life.

# Index

# Walking On Air

### How to face challenges with resilience and adversity with strength

### by Francis O' Toole

If you enjoyed this book, please post a review
on Amazon and Goodreads.

Thank you for your custom!

To contact the author/publisher, please email:
francismartinotoole@gmail.com

Printed in Great Britain
by Amazon